# THE JEWISH PROBLEM
# IN THE MODERN WORLD

## THE HOME UNIVERSITY LIBRARY
### OF MODERN KNOWLEDGE

### Editors

Rt. Hon. H. A. L. Fisher, O.M.,
F.R.S., LL.D., D.Litt.

Prof. Gilbert Murray, F.B.A.,
LL.D., D.Litt.

Dr. Julian S. Huxley,
F.R.S., M.A., D.Sc.

*For list of volumes in the Library
see end of book.*

# THE
# JEWISH PROBLEM
## IN THE
# MODERN WORLD

*By*
JAMES PARKES

LONDON
Thornton Butterworth Ltd

# THE
# JEWISH PROBLEM
# IN THE

*First Published* . . . . . . 1939

# CONTENTS

## PART I

## THE PRE-WAR WORLD

## PART II

## THE POST-WAR WORLD

# PART I
# THE PRE-WAR WORLD

## THE PRE-WAR WORLD

To the man who has no knowledge of
their history few present institutions seem
a mechanical enigma... scattered over most of
the world, or where more than a tiny fraction
of the population they have dispersed more
notice than many peoples far more numerous
than themselves. Why? Either they are in
their very nature a very abnormal people, or
they have had a very abnormal history.
The racial philosophers of to-day find the
explanation in the first alternative. They
ascribe to Jews peculiar and unalterable
qualities of blood, and from this inborn
origin they deduce a psychological other-
ness, which renders them a foreign body in
every community.

In so far as the physical transmission of
special and unique racial characteristics
is concerned, the theory that no scientific
justification. Our knowledge of 'race' is
still slight and the deductions which we can
make are still uncertain, but even if our know

# CHAPTER I

## WHY THERE IS A JEWISH QUESTION

To the man who has no knowledge of their history Jews present an insoluble, even a menacing, enigma. Scattered throughout the world, nowhere more than a tiny fraction of the population, they have received more notice than many peoples far more numerous than themselves. Why? Either they are in their very nature a very abnormal people, or they have had a very abnormal history. The racial philosophies of to-day find the explanation in the first alternative. They ascribe to Jews peculiar and unalterable qualities of blood, and from this physical origin they deduce a psychological "other-ness," which renders them a foreign body in every community.

In so far as the physical transmission of special and unique "racial" characteristics is concerned, the theory has no scientific justification. Our knowledge of "race" is still slight, and the deductions which we can make are still uncertain, but even if our knowledge were further advanced than it is, we could still say that " race " offered no explanation of the Jewish question. For, in the first place, in so far as Jews are " Semites," they are not the only members of this racial group ; and other Semites, such as the Arabs, show characteristics completely different from theirs ; and, in the second place, the Jews are by no means a pure racial group. They are as mixed as most other peoples in their origins, and just as drops of " Semitic " blood must flow in the veins of almost every European, so drops of blood of every other racial group flow in the veins of the " Semitic " Jews.

Because the ordinary man assumes that the Jews have passed through the same historical process as that of himself and his ancestors, he naturally ascribes the differences which he observes to some deliberate or unalterable characteristic, to something which he would say was " in the blood " even if he did not intend thereby to endorse any precise racial theory.

In actual fact there is a Jewish question not because of Jewish " blood," but because of Jewish history.

All peoples are largely the product of their history. British and German characteristics are extraordinarily different. But this does not make either the British or the Germans abnormal. For the differences are normal consequences of different histories, which in turn are normal developments of different geographical situations. The British, living on an island, have had a wonderful opportunity of building undisturbed sharply defined national characteristics and national institutions ; the Germans, placed in the middle of a continent, with no natural boundaries of their own and exposed to every movement of the nations, have been in exactly the opposite position. Just as the British and the German present the " normal " consequences of the position just described, so Jews are the normal product of their own history and geographical position.

It was inevitable that the people who inhabited a country which was the centre of the civilized world should have a special importance. And this was the position of Palestine in the centuries in which the main bulk of the Jewish people inhabited it. It was the bridge between the Mediterranean and Asia, between the civilizations of the Euphrates valley, the Nile valley, and the Mediterranean countries of Greece and Italy. The armies of every conqueror marched past it ; the influences of every civilization reached it. Jerusalem bowed her head in succession to the generals of Assyria, Persia, Greece, Egypt and Rome ; Jewish scholars and prophets drew inspiration from the religion and philosophy of the East, of Egypt and of Greece.

A people so exposed to the world, both politically and intellectually, had either to succumb, or to develop a strong individuality of its own, a capacity to absorb, and not be overwhelmed ; to meet every change of fortune and not be crushed. There are Jews in the world to-day because the Jews did not succumb to the consequences of their geographical position two thousand years ago. That one quality of pertinacity has ensured that they should not disappear since, and national pertinacity is not a sufficiently unusual quality to be called " abnormal." All that can be said is that the Jews have exhibited this quality through-out a most unusual history.

And yet even their pertinacity is not wholly an inexplicable enigma. They had the strongest known reason for it—the con-sciousness of a religious mission. The Jews of Palestine, living as they did at the meeting-point of the world's ideas, evolved an ethical religion, based on a link between the ideas of God and of morality, more definite and uncompromising than any of their neighbours. The longing for the knowledge of God, the seeking after righteousness of the Hebrew poets and prophets, far surpassed the ideas current among their neighbours, and took quite a different form amongst the Greeks. The feelings of privilege and responsibility which they drew from their religion were the basic causes of the survival of the Jews.

It was also the cause of friction with their neighbours, though it is wrong to call the hostility which Jews encountered in the ancient world " antisemitism." The friction arose from the fact that they were inevitably intolerant in a world which was completely tolerant in matters of religion. Jehovah had none of the accommodating characteristics of Jupiter or Venus. His worship was stern and puritanical, lacking the sensuous and sensual appeal of the rites of Greece or Asia. Moreover, this intolerance found official recognition, and brought an unexpected economic advantage. The Jews were excused participation in certain very onerous civic duties because they involved sacrifice. As they also involved heavy expenditure from the private pocket of the man concerned, wealthy Jews were the objects of a very natural jealousy.

When, in the fourth century A.D., the ancient world itself accepted an ethical and monotheistic religion, it might have been thought that such abnormality as there was in the Jewish position would disappear. But, as has been said, monotheism is intolerant, and the new faith, Christianity, was as intolerant as its parent.

Herein lies the basic cause of antisemitism, an intolerant minority under an intolerant majority. For neither could ignore the other entirely, since both claimed the monopoly of the interpretation of the same book—the Old Testament. Their interpretations were mutually inconsistent. If Christianity were right in seeing prophecies of the coming of Jesus of Nazareth as Messiah on all its pages, then Christianity might claim to be right in seeing there also the divine condemnation of the Jews. The Jews, by the interpretation of the early Church, were an utterly reprobate and rejected people, since they had rejected and killed their Messiah, and had not repented after His resurrection. It was an easy step to date this rejection to a still earlier period in their history and, as Christian interpretations of the Old Testament developed, their patriarchs and prophets were taken from them and made into " pre-incarnation Christians ; " all the promises and hopes on which they nourished their hearts during their long exile, were taken over by their rival, the Church. To them was allotted only the condemnation and the threat. Out of this false picture, gradually and unintentionally, a popular hatred and contempt for the Jews was born, the terrible social phenomenon which the modern world calls " anti-semitism."

This is the first real abnormality in their history ; that they were painted before their neighbours, not as they were in actual life, but as they were in one half of their own religious literature of a thousand years earlier.

All the promise and encouragement of the prophets were denied to them, all the purifying and purging which had taken place since the canon of the Old Testament was closed, was totally ignored—indeed the Church was totally unaware of it—and the Jew was held to be wholly and entirely described in the most violent denunciations of the prophets. And if in reality he did not conform to such a picture, that in itself was but the malice and the deception of the devil.

Religious in origin, antisemitism soon took more prosaic forms, and the first penalty to which the intolerant majority condemned the stiff-necked minority was the most crushing from which the Jew has ever suffered. In the Roman world the Jew had been a citizen at first of Palestine, then of the Roman Empire when in the beginning of the third century A.D. citizenship was extended to all peoples within its wide frontiers. But in a Europe where every civic act was part of a Christian religious ceremony, there was no equality for the Jew, indeed no place for him at all. He lost his citizenship and, although a permanent and settled resident, became a tolerated alien. Here is the second abnormality.

From the tenth century to the nineteenth for the Jews in Western Europe, from the tenth to the twentieth for the much larger numbers in its Eastern half, Jews had no share in the gradual evolution of political responsibility, no rights of citizenship, no security of tenure, no legal existence except by the whim of an owner who could dispose of them as he pleased. It is recorded of a medieval bishop that on obtaining possession of certain cities he found that there were Jews amongst their inhabitants. Not wishing to possess any Jews he ordered them all to be burnt. Less grim in her attitude was a French abbess who found that there were two of the Jews of Louis IX (Saint Louis) on her domains. Moved by religious feelings similar to those of the bishop she wrote to the king and requested him either to have them immediately baptized or to remove them. Rightlessness could scarcely go further.

Close on the heels of this second abnormality comes the third. The Jew owed his permission to reside in any city to the will of its prince. The mere fact of being within his dominions made him the absolute property of the latter—except where princes made agreements with each other that none would steal the other's Jews. The prince expected a return for granting the privilege of residence. From the twelfth century onwards the return usually took the form of making the Jew a royal usurer. On the one hand the gradual extension of Christendom to the control of every act of life excluded the Jew first from the tenure of land, then from the artisan and commercial gilds, and on the other the royal charters by which he lived encouraged, and at times compelled, him to practise usury.

The reasons for this are complex. It is usually said that the basic reason was the fact that usury was prohibited to Christians. So it was, but rabbinic law also frowned upon it among Jews. Moreover, the fact that it was prohibited does not mean that no Christian practised it. Murder and adultery were also prohibited, but they were somewhat freely practised throughout the Middle Ages. Again it is said that the Jew took to usury because of an inherited talent for the financial profession. This is even less true. There is no evidence whatever that the Jew was always a successful financier. When the profession began to be common in the twelfth century all the evidence shows that it was in a very experimental state, and the basis on which it was worked was thoroughly amateurish.

The moneylenders of early Europe were all those, whether Christian or Jew, who had money. Much of society, both rich and poor, saw little of actual coin in daily life. In the twelfth century the extension of civilization brought great new demands for actual coin. The class of borrowers grew rapidly, and lenders increased likewise. As the century saw, for the same reason, a great extension of commerce, merchants came to be the chief lenders, for coin naturally passed through their hands.

Though they were never so wealthy or so powerful as the great merchant gilds of Italy, Flanders or the Hanse towns, the Jews were largely a merchant community. In the natural course of events, they thus took their place among the moneylenders. What gave them an unwelcome prominence was no inherited ability, but the fact that they and all their goods were the property of the most permanently impecunious class of society— the princes.

Under the medieval system, by which princes received many services but few taxes, and were expected to support much of the expenses of national administrations out of the revenues of their own private lands, this permanent poverty was almost universal. Under such conditions the possession of a community of individuals capable of producing a considerable yield of actual coin was a privilege not lightly to be foregone. Jews were an asset to the treasury, and their activities were part of the financial system of the Crown and dictated by its needs, rather than part of the machinery of a normal economic system. This is shown by the way in which maximum permitted rates of usury followed the need of the royal exchequer, not the rules of commercial supply and demand.

In the middle of the fourteenth century, Jews and other usurers in France were compelled to reduce their usury in rural areas from twopence to a penny per week per pound (from $43\frac{1}{3}$ per cent. to $21\frac{2}{3}$ per cent.) owing to the appalling poverty of the peasants. In 1360, when the peasants had been still further impoverished by wars, pestilence and bad harvests, usury was suddenly increased to fourpence ($86\frac{2}{3}$ per cent.) because the Crown had to raise enormous sums to pay the English the ransom demanded for the King, John the Good, who had been taken prisoner at the Battle of Poitiers.

All medieval evidence agrees that, as a usurer, the Jew was preferable to the Christian. But this did not make him into a public benefactor. The enormous rates of interest which were demanded not merely by the insecurity of the times, but even more by the continual necessity of replenishing the royal treasuries, caused the ruin of innumerable debtors, and made the Jewish usurers the most detested class in Europe.

It might be thought that the two facts, that all merchants lent money, and that the

Christian usurers were universally found to be worse than the Jewish, would have meant that the idea " usurer " would not have been linked almost exclusively to the word " Jew," as, in fact, it was. Though, as a matter of history, the two groups of Italian merchants who were primarily known in Northern Europe for their financial activities, the Lombards and the Cahorsin, were as much detested as the Jews, yet the reason is not far to seek why the word stuck to the Jews and not to any Christian group. Though all Jews were not usurers a large proportion were. Though Christian usurers were worse, only a small proportion of Christians practised usury. Jew and usurer could be identified in the popular mind ; Christian and usurer could not. So there passed into the sub-conscious memory of Europe the idea that the Jew, already considered the enemy of God, was also the enemy of society. This was the third abnormality.

There was nothing in the position of the Jew which was likely to break down these two beliefs. While individual Christian scholars might hold the friendliest discussions with Jewish scholars, the Church as a whole was unremitting in her hostility and her condemnation. In theological works and popular mystery plays, in picture, in glass and sculpture she held him up to execration. She set him apart from Christian society by imposing on him a special dress, and later, special ghettoes in which he was compelled to live. Popular superstition enriched what official teaching sanctioned. The Jew was believed to seek Christian blood for ritual purposes, and to steal and murder Christian children for these needs ; he was believed to poison wells and spread diseases ; and all the time rumours spread from land to land that he was in league with the Saracens, with the Tartars, with all the enemies of Christendom. In the popular memory of Europe he was more than merely an economic scourge ; he was a malignant foe, seeking ever to destroy both body and soul of the Christian enemy.

To its honour the Papacy countenanced none of these extravagances. It tempered justice with the extreme of severity, but it set its face continually against the accusation of ritual murder or of poisoning of wells. It designed to keep the Jew in a condition of humiliation, but within that condition it considered that he should enjoy physical security.

The three abnormalities already described

would be enough in themselves to explain what is peculiar in the Jewish people ; but there is more to come. These were abnormalities imposed from without ; they inevitably provoked a reaction on the internal life of the Jewish communities and the psychology of the individual Jew.

It has been said that the privileges which the Jew enjoyed under the pagan Roman Empire caused friction between him and his pagan neighbour, but this must not be taken to mean that Jews, as is sometimes said, lived on permanently bad terms with their non-Jewish surroundings. The clearest evidence of this is the long struggle which the Church had to undertake during the first thousand years of its life to preserve Christian clergy and laity from the influence of Judaism and from friendship with Jews. During this thousand years there were examples in both east and west of outbreaks against local Jewish communities, but they were due to the particularly ferocious piety of individuals. They were not caused by general hostility and their duration was short-lived. But as the Middle Ages advanced the effects of the abnormalities already mentioned began to be felt in a general lowering of the popular estimate of the Jews. The religious enthusiasm of the First Crusade in 1096 was widely manifested in massacres of Jews. In the centuries which followed any excuse was enough to move the populace against them. The fantastic charges already mentioned, that they murdered Christian children for ritual purposes, that they caused the pestilence which devastated the insanitary cities of the period by poisoning the wells, that they stole and stabbed the sacred wafers from the Churches, causing them to bleed, these and similar accusations were universally believed against them.

The hostility of the mob inevitably bred a corresponding attitude among the Jews. Hatred and contempt are group sentiments most certain to be paid in kind, and medieval Jewry was no exception to the rule. In spite of the universalism and tolerance explicit in much Jewish teaching, Judaism, as the centuries advanced, could not but become narrower and more intolerant. This was the more natural in that persecution, even when purely economic in origin, always found a religious excuse and justification. It was in the name of Christ and the Virgin Mary that the Jews were killed and tortured: the attitude of Jews to the doctrines and practices of the Faith which so treated

24

them was, and often still is, what might be expected.

Even more profound in their effect on Jewish mentality were the perpetual fear and the insecurity within which life was lived in a medieval community. From the thirteenth century onwards the story of the Jews is an almost unrelieved chronicle of massacres, false accusations, confiscations and expulsions. Bribery was the only weapon in the armoury of Jewish defence ; moneylending the only method to secure the ammunition. Forbidden to carry arms, deprived of legal rights, the Jew could do nothing but cringe before his enemy, and seek for gold and ever more gold to appease him. Such a life, lived for centuries, can only have a thoroughly deleterious effect on the social psychology of the victims.

The Jews found their compensation within the walls of their houses. At first they had voluntarily lived together, as had every other " national " group in the polyglot communities which formed the cities of the Roman Empire. Later residence in the ghetto was compulsory. Herded together in quarters which often prevented any natural increase of the community, they found in the intellectual world compensations for the humiliations and dangers of the Christian world outside.

To the intellectual activities of medieval Jewry Christian Europe owes much. Capable of understanding and interpreting the science, mathematics, botany, astronomy and geography of the Arabic world, they played an important, if unacknowledged, part in the growth of medieval culture. Above all they reintroduced to European scholarship the philosophy of Aristotle, who was known to the medieval world only in Arabic translations. As time went on, and the outer world grew more unbearable, interest in " secular " studies diminished. Interminable argument on the minutiæ of religious observances took their place, and the Jew fled from the bitterness of this world into a world entirely his own, compounded of never-ending legal distinctions and a fantastic and unhealthy mysticism. Great scholars dwindled into narrow pedants ; rabbis often sank from being the most enlightened religious teachers of Europe into little better than quacks and witch-doctors.

The process of decay took centuries, and it would be utterly false to give the impression that the final result was either total or universal in its collapse, but it must be remembered that the " Middle Ages " for the Jew lasted from the tenth century until the nineteenth. The Renaissance entirely passed them by, and even among the small Jewish communities of Western Europe, this life of artificial restrictions and hectic intellectual compensation passed away less than one hundred and fifty years ago.

To complete the picture one crowning abnormality forces itself upon our attention : the abnormality of geographic distribution. In so far as *voluntary* movements are concerned there has been nothing abnormal in Jewish history. In the early centuries of their national life the Jews were far more stay-at-home than most of the peoples living on the fringes of the Mediterranean. Unlike their Semitic neighbours of the coast or of the desert, their ambition was to sit every man under his own vine, eating the figs of his own fig tree. Trade attracted them but little, and it is only with the economic decline of the Kingdoms of Judah and Israel that it became normal to find worshippers of Jahwe among the caravans and in the trading centres which had developed along the coasts of the Mediterranean, Arabia and India, and had spread overland as far as China. Solomon had to go to the maritime empire of Tyre to get seamen for his fleet. The prophets knew practically nothing of Jewish traders ; but, by the first century of the Christian era, Jews had drifted, with their neighbours of the coast and the commercial cities of Syria, into most of the great marts of the Roman Empire.

They followed all the normal occupations of the urban population of the Empire. They became conspicuous economically only when the Mohammedan conquest of the southern and eastern shores of the Mediterranean closed the markets of Syria and Africa to the Syrian Christian merchants. Their penetration into the hinterland of Europe was slow. They followed the line of the cities up the Rhone, down the Seine, and across to the Loire on the west and the Rhine on the east.

In the year five hundred there would probably have been no city with a Jewish community which did not also contain communities of Syrians, Greeks and Italians. But by the year eleven hundred the other communities, except in some respects those from Italy, had been absorbed into the rest of the population. There was no religious difference to separate them, and they were cut off from their old home-lands, now partly under Moslem rule. In such circumstances the mere presence of Jews assumed a significance it had not hitherto possessed. It became natural to think of them as aliens, often as the only aliens, in an otherwise homogeneous group.

As Jews became more and more concentrated into commercial and financial occupations, they tended to spread through the new merchant cities which sprang up in the north of Europe in the twelfth and thirteenth centuries. This was a voluntary dispersion. It was soon followed by involuntary ones. The march of the Crusading armies, as has already been mentioned, was often marked by massacres of Jews. As the armies moved from the west of Europe to the south-east, the Jew fled to the north-east, into eastern Germany, Bohemia and especially Poland. Close on the heels of a dispersion due to flight came dispersions due to expulsions. In early days enthusiastic princes or bishops had sometimes offered their Jews the alternatives of baptism or departure. The Jews who were affected by such orders were few, and they probably never had far to move. But in 1290 the whole community of English Jews was expelled, and during the succeeding centuries mass emigrations, on a scale almost comparable to the flight from Germany and Austria to-day, took place from France, from cities and states of Central Europe, and culminated in the terrible expulsion from

Spain and Portugal in the last decade of the fifteenth century.

The distribution of the Jews in Europe is thus almost entirely the result of external causes. By the end of the eighteenth century only one group of communities could point to a relatively continuous and undisturbed career. These were the small communities of Italy, which had been in the peninsula for close on two thousand years. The other great Jewish communities of the Roman Empire, those of France and Spain, had vanished, the latter entirely, and the former everywhere except from a few cities of the south. In the same way the great medieval communities of Western Europe had dwindled almost to nothing. English medieval Jewry had left no descendants on the island ; German Jews survived in parts of Alsace (a French province since Louis XIV) and as " tolerated " groups in a number of cities, strictly limited in numbers and occupations.

In place of these Jewries two movements, one from the south-west one from the north-east, had created new settlements, often on the old positions. The flight from Spain had spread the Spanish Jews not only into the Balkans, the Levant, and the cities of northern Africa, but had gradually created important new Jewish communities in Holland, England and the commercial cities bordering the Atlantic from Hamburg to Bayonne. A century later troubles in Poland started the first return movements towards the West from the immense reservoirs of European Jewry which medieval persecution had gradually caused to accumulate along the Russian frontier. " German " and " Polish " Jews began to appear in the eighteenth century in most of the cities and territories where " Spanish " Jews were already established.

In their wealth and standing the Jewries of the eighteenth century differed considerably. The " Spanish " Jews were generally respected ; the " German " Jews as generally despised. But neither were free ; both were subject to arbitrary discrimination, both excluded from the land ; hence both followed their traditional occupations of merchant and financier, the one on a large scale and the other on a small.

# CHAPTER II

## THE EMANCIPATION OF THE JEWS

It has already been said that the Middle Ages lasted for the Jews, even in Western Europe, right into the nineteenth century. The élite of the Jewish communities of a few great cities won social recognition and toleration a couple of hundred years earlier, and a handful of Jews were welcome in the cultured homes of London, Berlin and Amsterdam at a period when the mass of the Jewish population was still sunk in medieval conditions, and living in a world of medieval thought and superstition.

Jews in the United States of America were the first to enter into the rights and duties of citizenship, as a consequence of the American Revolution. The French Revolution, which followed so shortly after it, set the example for their emancipation in Europe. In the Napoleonic period which succeeded it, the emancipation of the Jews was carried out wherever French hegemony was established. But as soon as Napoleon fell, reaction set in in, and though the Bourbons made no change in France itself, the only other country which repealed none of the pro-Jewish measures was Holland. In Germany the attitude of the different states varied enormously. Lübeck and Bremen expelled their communities entirely. In the greater part of the country they were reduced to their former status of tolerated aliens, though there was a perceptible improvement in their actual condition, whatever their legal position. Elsewhere they remained subject to abnormal legislation until the middle of the nineteenth century; and it was not until the second half that full emancipation was attained. In legal terms England was one of the last countries to remove all disabilities, but the reason lay less in anti-Jewish feeling than in the fact that for practical purposes all disadvantages had disappeared at an earlier period.

In so far as constitutional measures were concerned, reform ebbed and flowed with the success and failure of the revolutionary movements which were a feature of the century. Revolution meant whole or partial emancipation; reaction meant an attempt to return to medieval conditions. This fact is of considerable importance for the understanding of nineteenth-century Jewish history. Decisions

33          B

to emancipate the Jews were taken on the basis of a political theory and were not due to any particular sympathy with the Jews themselves. It was neither a feeling of pity for the victims of centuries of Christian intolerance, nor a recognition that the Jews were especially worthy of better treatment than they had so far received, which led to it, but a general and theoretical conception of human equality which rejected the necessity for an exception in the midst of society.

So far as the general public were concerned there was no widespread desire that the Jew should be granted equality ; the old hatreds, the old contempt, the old superstitions were as active as they had ever been. So far also as the mass of the Jews were concerned, there was no desire to leave the old paths. Accustomed to the strange life which they had lived for centuries within the ghetto walls, they had come, in spite of their inevitable contacts with it, to view the world outside with alarm rather than desire. In particular the rabbis and the elders of the communities feared the effects which emancipation might have on the younger generation. They were alarmed lest their loyalty to the traditional ways of their fathers should weaken before the temptations of the two worlds now open to them, one Christian, one sceptical and pagan, both hostile and both dangerously seductive.

A generation sufficed to change the attitude of a large proportion of the individual Jews affected. But the very rapidity of this change assured the survival of the traditional attitude on the part of the rest of the population on the one hand, and fulfilled the fears of the rabbis on the other.

The old world of Judaism had been slowly and laboriously built up during centuries of the artificial life of a community rigidly segregated from its neighbours. This segregation had had its origin in the desire of the Jews themselves to maintain their religious beliefs and observances uncontaminated by pagan influences ; it had been continued by the legislative action of Christian powers fearing Jewish influence ; and it had been consummated by the deepest barrier of all, if the most undefinable, the barrier of mutual suspicion, hatred and contempt.

Its forms and customs were ill-adapted to the new age ; it lacked elasticity and adaptability ; it was a whole whose parts were locked together ; and there was no recognized centre from which new and authoritative modifications could come. The inevitable result was a break-away from Judaism on the part of those who caught the spirit of the new age. The mother of Disraeli was typical of many Western Jews in her contempt for Judaism and her determination to see her son baptized.

The tension was accentuated by the fact that only a minority of the Jewish people living between the years 1800 and 1900 ever lived in " the nineteenth century." Emancipation only affected the Jews of Western Europe ; but even they had for some time previously been accustomed to look with respect on the Jews of Poland as the source for their religious teachers and rabbis : and the Jews of Poland were still living in the Middle Ages, untouched by the new stirrings in the West.

It was only slowly that a *via media* appeared in Judaism and Jewish communal organizations whereby they could adapt themselves to the new circumstances. By the middle of the century new congregations with reformed or modified ritual were beginning to organize themselves out of the individual pioneers of the previous generation. Distinctions of dress, appearance and custom were quietly dropped, and externally the western Jews took on wholly the life and manners of western non-Jewish society.

By the second half of the century they had become acutely conscious of the difference between themselves and eastern European Jews, and the stream which had previously flowed from east to west in terms of piety and scholarship, began to flow from west to east in terms of secular education, political intercession and constructive charity.

These changes were immensely aided by one of the most important activities born of emancipation : an interest in Jewish history. It is curious that the successors of those who wrote the incomparable historical narratives of the Old Testament lost all skill in historical writing. Until the middle of the nineteenth century all attempts to write the post-biblical history of the Jews in any continuous or systematic fashion had been made by Christians. But in the 1830's there began in Germany a long line of distinguished Jewish historians, whose work was of great importance to the Jews themselves in that it enabled them to see their own history in a general setting, and to understand the part which they had played or been made to play in European evolution. Seeing themselves in this way for the first time they saw themselves as others saw them, and realized both the strength and the weakness of the communal life and thought which their fathers had evolved. At first the weakness was more apparent than the strength, and this explains the rapidity of the individual transformation of the Jews affected.

The same reason explains the reaction which followed their appearance. Though an act of legislation had made them into normal citizens, it could not make them into normal individuals. They were plunged suddenly into the whirl of nineteenth-century life with the inheritance of other centuries still clinging to them. And the nineteenth century was the century above all others which gave them the fullest scope both to take advantage of and to suffer from the abnormalities which the past had bequeathed them.

It was a century in which established ideas in politics, religion and science were criticized in the market-place, as in the eighteenth they had been in the *salons* of a few aristocratic dilettanti. The Jews, with the intellectual but narrow tradition of centuries of rabbinic discussion behind them, quickly took their place among the most able analysts of contemporary life, but their strength lay far more in destructive than in constructive analysis. Their quick wits, their clever tongues could pull to pieces the surviving medievalisms of church, society and state. Logic could do this, but logic alone could not rebuild. A revolution can break with the past : evolution is an organic growth, and needs a profound insight into, and knowledge of, the reasons for the old order ; an insight and a knowledge which Jews, who had had no part in it, could only slowly acquire. But from the beginning they criticized—and the slower witted representatives of the old order not unnaturally resented their criticisms.

In the changing order of the nineteenth century their criticisms had an added sting for those whose power was passing. Jews had come to be almost exclusively town-dwellers, and in particular their largest communities were in those great cities of commerce and manufacture whose importance increased rapidly all through the century. There they were at the centre of every movement, their fingers on the pulse of every development. But not only were they town-dwellers in the first century of an almost entirely urban civilization, but they were most numerous in just those groups which were rapidly rising through prominence to the control of political and national life. For they were members of the middle classes, first as merchants and financiers, then (as the

39

educational systems were opened to their children) as lawyers, doctors and journalists.

Not only were there new cities and a new class ready to receive them, there were new political movements which possessed none of the prejudices of the older aristocracy, but which accepted their criticisms and welcomed their co-operation. The nineteenth century was the century of constitutional radicalism, of liberalism and individualism—all the movements in which Jews found themselves most at home. It was natural that they should play their part in these parties, for it was to the great ideas of the French Revolution and the idealism which preceded it that they owed their emancipation ; it was to liberalism and " the Manchester School " that they owed the removal of the bars to their economic advancement ; and in the new spirit of social reform, and the new demands of social justice, they found a field of practical activity for which the deepest principles of their rabbinic inheritance had admirably prepared them.

In the world of business and finance also the ground was excellently fitted for their entrance. It was a century of unparalleled economic development, of universal financial expansion, of audacious and experimental speculation. For such a world they were much better fitted than the older possessors of wealth. To the ordinary national the acquisition of wealth had meant above all security and the possibility of founding a family. The great titles in the England of the nineteenth century belonged largely to the descendants of the great merchants of the sixteenth and succeeding centuries. The gambler was the exception; the ideal was careful investment, the acquisition of a place in "society," and a solid fortune in land and sound securities to bequeath to an heir.

Such a class was slow to seize the risky opportunities for making money which the new age offered. But the attitude of the Jew to money was inevitably different, for a very simple reason. It had never possessed for him its basic, most essential quality for the Christian—the gift of security. In extremity it could at best secure a respite from an order of expulsion, from an act of violence or injustice; it could not do more; and even to do that it had to be expended lavishly, rapidly and with the recklessness of a gambler. Money represented the possibility of the immediate purchase of something worth while, and very little more.

41

It is important to understand this, for the long association of the Jews with money has created a totally false association of ideas in the minds of many people, who consider that money is their main interest, that they have a "racial" genius in acquiring it, that they hoard it and love it for its own sake. As social security advanced, a small class of rich Jews settled down to be landed proprietors like their Christian friends ; and there have, of course, been Jewish misers and Jewish financial wizards, but all these are rare exceptions. The conventional Jewish attitude to money is that it is something to use for a desirable end, something not very important in itself with which one can play. Although rich men bought power in the Jewish community as in every other, Jewish admiration has nearly always been given to learning rather than to wealth. In medieval Jewish chronicles it is common to find pious ejaculations of gratitude to the Almighty for having put so much money in the hands of His people, but the reason given by the chroniclers is that it could be spent for their preservation, that the bribes which they could give to their owners enabled them to remain faithful to their religion. But there is not to be found in their pages complaints in the manner of

Shylock that so much money is wasted for bribes, that so much is stolen from them, so much lost by monstrous taxation.

For a people with such a philosophy of money this century offered an interminable succession of opportunities. Much was wasted on fantastic speculation by every nation, there were many financial scandals ; but the bulk of it was used with far-sighted daring in the building up of the new industrial and commercial civilization. And in this process Jewish capital played an amazingly large part. Without the imagination of the Rothschilds, of Sir David Salomons who founded the first Joint-Stock Bank, and of many other Jewish groups and individuals, the development of railways, canals, steamship lines, and mines would have proceeded far more slowly than it did.

One final characteristic the Jew possessed which was of greater service to him in this century than it had ever been before. He was dispersed through all the important centres of trade, finance and commerce at a moment when, largely through the development of British industries, all these occupations were becoming cosmopolitan. He had no inhibitions about " foreigners," no fears of foreign countries. He was prepared to set up a branch of his business in Rio de Janeiro or Shanghai, to invest his money in America or Africa. Language and frontier were not barriers to him ; commercial adventure had no terrors for him, and while the Rothschilds from their offices in London, Paris, or Vienna sent their agents all over the world, Jewish pedlars, their packs on their backs, or their whole worldly possessions in a wagon, followed the American pioneers across the great plains of the Middle West, and the first shops and first dealers in many Middle Western towns were Jews who had been born half-way across the world in the still medieval ghettoes of Russia and Eastern Europe.

The same qualities urged on both the millionaire in his office and the pedlar on the dusty roads—imagination, the power of improvisation, the willingness to take risks.

It is no wonder that Jews needed but few years to be completely at home in the life of the nineteenth century. It was a century " made for them," and they assimilated themselves completely to it. What few realized, including the Jews themselves, was how superficial this assimilation often was. The nineteenth century was not, in fact, a wholly new world. It was linked by innumerable invisible threads to earlier times, it was upheld and held back by innumerable traditions ; it had inherited prejudices and special ways of thought ; its fruit ripened from the sap of that past in which the Jew had had no share. Hesitations and reluctances on the part of the Christian were meaningless and illogical to him, inexplicable and irrational. In fairness it must be added that the impatience, the radicalism, the perpetual destructive and sometimes contemptuous criticism of the society of which he had become a member, were displayed as vigorously in his attacks upon his own traditions, upon the precise observations of Jewish orthodoxy, the meticulous obedience to rabbinical ceremonial prescriptions, as in anything which he directed against the Christian churches or Christian society. And on the other hand, he shared these attitudes with non-Jewish critics of society as vigorous as himself.

These gaps in the completeness of his identification of himself with the communities of nineteenth-century Europe passed unobserved or un-understood by his contemporaries. Those who drew attention to them did so on the basis that they were proof of the deliberate and wanton malice of the Jew ; the reasons which explained, and to a considerable extent excused, the Jewish critics were outside their comprehension.

Curiously enough it was not the justice of their complaints, but the general success of Jewish assimilation which gave to their attacks what force they possessed. For Jews had assimilated themselves so successfully in appearance, that it was only the Jewish malefactor who stood out as a Jew. The period was not really " Jew-conscious " and did not notice a Jew until he was pointed out. If a man was a normally decent citizen it was a matter of total indifference whether he were Jewish or not. Even in the conservative circles of governments and hereditary aristocracies there was scarcely a barrier which the waters of baptism could not wash away. One of the most interesting examples of this fact is the almost total disappearance of the Spanish Jewish families which returned to England under Cromwell. By the nineteenth century they had vanished by baptism and marriage into the general English community.

The brilliance and variety of the contribution which Jews made to nineteenth-century civilization thus passed completely unnoticed, and was never placed to their credit. When the smallness of the Jewish communities of Europe is considered, their contribution to the great names of the period is astounding. They come from every country, and from every walk of life. In the list which follows some are half-Jews, some were baptized in infancy or later in life, but all were wholly or partly children or grandchildren of the ghetto, whose contribution, in all probability, the world would never have received had it not been for the emancipation of the Jews.

In politics there were, in England Disraeli, in Germany, Stahl, a founder of the Conservative Party, and Lassalle, the pioneer of Trade Unionism ; in France Crémieux, one of the greatest figures of the Second Republic, and one of the men called back in his old age to save France after the downfall of Napoleon in 1870 ; in Italy Luigi Luzzatti, the greatest of her liberal Prime Ministers.

In letters there is Francis Turner Palgrave, compiler of the ever-popular " Golden Treasury " ; Sidney Lee and Israel Gollancz, the Shakespearean scholars ; Israel Zangwill and Bret Harte ; Pinero, author of *The Second Mrs. Tanqueray* and *Trelawney of the Wells* ; and, above all, the poet Heine.

On the stage there are Sarah Bernhardt and Beerbohm Tree ; in music, Mendelssohn, Meyerbeer, Offenbach ; in painting, Solomon J. Solomon and Camille Pissarro ; in journalism Jews created five of the great dailies of the world (though only one of them is still in Jewish hands), in Vienna the *Neue Freie Presse*, in Germany the *Berliner Tageblatt* and the *Frankfurter Zeitung*, in England the *Daily Telegraph*, and in America the *New York Times*.

In science and medicine their contributions, though from men whose names are unknown to the ordinary public, have been equally remarkable, but it is more surprising to find that Jews played also important parts in the pioneering work on the photograph, the telephone, the motor-car, wireless and the microphone. And few who use a *Singer* sewing machine reflect that it is a Jewish gift to the housewife.

In public service they have been equally conspicuous. The International Institute of Agriculture, and the Royal Society for the Prevention of Cruelty to Animals ; Dr. Barnardo's Homes, the Wandsworth Orphanages, the Children's Hospital in Westminster, the Julius Rosenwald schools and institutes for the negro in America, all these owe their existence to the initiative of individual Jews or men of Jewish extraction, and to these it may be added that it is said that General Booth, founder of the Salvation Army, was of Jewish descent.

The list makes no pretence whatever to completeness. What, however, is as important as their number is the fact that the ordinary man would hardly have thought of any of the people concerned as Jewish. He would have considered them English, French, German, Italian or American. The fact that they were Jews would not have interested him.

What is true of the great names here presented is equally true of the general mass of the Jewish population, the lawyers, doctors, business men, shopkeepers and artisans, or the tailors, bakers, boxers, singers and musicians, who form the bulk of the Jewish population. Except when some special occurrence drew attention to the fact, few of their neighbours were conscious that they were Jews. To all outward appearances their assimilation was complete.

## CHAPTER III

### THE REBIRTH OF ANTISEMITISM

It was the prevailing belief of the nineteenth century that prejudice against the Jews, where it still survived, was but the relic of a vanishing medievalism, and that the enlightenment of the age, and the assimilation of citizens of the Jewish faith, would soon write *finis* to a long and sad story of ignorance and fanaticism. One event, more than any other, shattered this illusion.

Towards the end of September 1894 a document reached the French War Ministry which revealed that a French officer was selling military secrets to Germany. Suspicion, which in the light of subsequent knowledge resembles prejudice rather than evidence, fell on the one Jewish officer on the general staff, Captain Alfred Dreyfus. On the 15th of October he was arrested, and on the 22nd of December he was condemned by a military court to degradation and deportation to a penal settlement. His degradation on the 5th of January was the scene of a furious demonstration not against him personally but against " the Jews," which had been prepared by a campaign of appalling virulence in the small but vocal press of the extreme Right and clerical parties.

On the 15th of March 1895 Dreyfus arrived at the penal settlement off French Guiana known as *les Iles de Salut*. In April he was transferred from the general prison to a specially constructed hut on Devil's Island, a rocky islet where he lived in complete isolation until the summer of 1899. Meanwhile, in France the excitement had not died down with the condemnation and disappearance of the prisoner. Many were troubled by irregularities in his trial, by his continual avowals of his innocence, and by the lack of motive for his treason, for Dreyfus was a married man with children, possessed a considerable private fortune, and lived quietly without any expensive vices. His family worked unremittingly to re-establish his innocence, but the mass of the public— quite naturally—could not believe that a Minister of War and a court of his brother officers could condemn to the horrors of public degradation and a life sentence under the most appalling conditions, an officer of whose guilt there were not the most irrefutable proofs.

It was not until the autumn of 1896 that new evidence came to hand to assist the party working for Dreyfus. The trial itself had been irregular, for evidence had been handed to the judges which was not communicated to the prisoner or his advocate ; but it was only when this evidence itself appeared to be suspicious that a movement in his favour began to grow. In November 1897 Matthew Dreyfus, his brother, was sufficiently sure of his ground to accuse another officer publicly of the authorship of the document which was the sole real basis of the accusation against Dreyfus. This officer, whose reputation for debts and fast living made him a much more likely criminal, was the Commandant Esterhazy. In spite of convincing proofs of his guilt—which was later established beyond all question—Esterhazy was unanimously acquitted in January 1898.

From this point onwards the struggle was a straight political issue between the army and the radicals, between the antisemites and the intellectuals. The one side was determined that, whatever the purely judicial position, the acceptance of the guilt of Dreyfus was the essential basis of patriotism, and of loyalty to the army ; the other side, at first merely convinced that the trial had been irregular, was now wholly convinced of the innocence of Dreyfus and the deliberate antisemitism of his condemnation.

Immediately after the acquittal of Esterhazy, Émile Zola, one of the greatest figures in the French world of letters, addressed a public letter to the President of the Republic which has become immortal under the title which Clemenceau gave it :

## J'ACCUSE !

Amidst scenes of violent excitement Zola was condemned for libelling the army, and fled to England. But the effect of his public accusation could not be removed, and in the year 1898 events succeeded one another with rapidity. The Army chiefs were still prepared to go to any extent to cover their initial blunder, but the suicide of their main instrument, Captain Henry, at a moment when he was under arrest for forgery in connexion with the affair, was more than in their tottering condition they could support. In October the Court of Appeal accepted a demand of Madame Dreyfus for the re-trial of her husband, and the verdict of the Court Martial of 1894 was quashed on June 3, 1899. Dreyfus was returned under escort to France, and arrived on the 1st of July.

A new court-martial met at Rennes on the 7th of August, and after a month of deliberation, pronounced their verdict. To cover the army, rather than to conform to any evidence which they had heard, they again found Dreyfus guilty by five votes to two, but, owing to "extenuating circumstances," reduced his sentence to ten years' detention in France.

Such a sentence could not be a permanent decision, since it corresponded to the needs neither of those who believed him guilty nor of those who asserted his innocence. If guilty there could be no such thing as extenuating circumstances for such a crime ; if innocent any punishment was unjust. The government attempted to cut the Gordian knot by a private message to Dreyfus that an appeal to the President would immediately be met with a pardon. After much hesitation Dreyfus accepted, partly to restore his health shattered by the ghastly rigours of Devil's Island, partly to be free to work for his complete acquittal.

Nearly seven years were to pass before the final scene of the drama. In July 1906, the supreme Court of Appeal pronounced Dreyfus completely vindicated, and restored to him his rank in the army.

Into the drama of the *Affaire Dreyfus* there entered before the end far more than the Jewish question. But the fact that Dreyfus was a Jew explains the lightheartedness with which his guilt was accepted by the chiefs of the army, and the violence with which those who believed in his innocence were attacked. If in the end it was not Jewish protestation, but the conscience of the French nation which after twelve years of struggle secured, indeed insisted on, his acquittal, even so it remains the classical example of the blind hate with which antisemitism could still move large masses of people, even in an enlightened age.

The reason why the nineteenth century witnessed such a renewal of a temper associated rather with the Middle Ages, is to be found primarily in the part played by the Jews in the economic expansion which followed the Napoleonic wars. Then was realized the immensity of the fortune acquired in no more than a single generation by the House of Rothschild. Five brothers working in co-operation from London, Vienna, Paris, Naples and Frankfurt, controlled a financial power rarely, if ever, possessed by private individuals. In actual fact the international political influence of the Rothschilds was slight, for the London and Paris Houses were influenced by the liberal ideas of the British and French Governments, and the Viennese and Neapolitan Houses by the autocratic ideas of those countries. But that did not alter the fact that their power in the money-markets of Europe was tremendous, and if they did not change the destinies of continents, they altered the destinies of many individuals. While there is little evidence that they were more unscrupulous than other Jewish or Christian financiers of the period, they were more successful ; and ruined rivals were ready to curse *the Jews* when overreached by the Rothschilds.

It was in France, during the reign of Louis-Philippe (1830–48) and the Second Republic which followed it, that the power of finance in the new bourgeois-industrial civilization was most strikingly visible. Plutocracy ruled everywhere, and the scandals of financial speculation were innumerable in quantity and vast in extent. Since the head of the French House of Rothschild was the most powerful financier in the country, all the forces of reaction against the new civilization, whether clerical and religious, aristocratic or proletarian, identified their enemy with "the Jews." But it is interesting to find that the author of one of the earliest attacks upon the emancipated Jews of the nineteenth century, A. Toussenel, exclaims in his introduction :

"But bear it in mind : whoever says ' Jew ' says ' Protestant.' The Englishman, the Dutchman, the Genevese, who read the will of God in the same book as the Jew, profess for the laws of equity and the rights of workers the same contempt as the Jew. There is even a rivalry between these races to establish which is the most avaricious and the most covetous."

And in fact he was right to this extent that these three nations were the leaders in the race for wealth, and, with the single exception of the Rothschilds, were far more powerful than any Jewish group, and no exception need be introduced in saying that they were all equally unscrupulous in their pursuit.

Toussenel wrote *The Jews, the Lords of the Age* in 1844. In 1848 a new turn was given to the antisemitic movement by the prominence of the Jews in the various revolutionary outbreaks of that year. While the Rothschilds had nothing to gain from them, the new Jewish middle class identified their interests extensively with the revolutionaries. In

France one of the most prominent figures in French Jewry, Adolphe Crémieux, became Minister of Justice of the new republican government. In Germany twenty Jews fell among the victims of the street-fighting in Berlin, and Gabriel Riesser, the protagonist of emancipation—for the Jews in Germany had not yet the equality of rights which they possessed in France—was the Vice-president of the " Constituent Assembly " which was to provide a constitution for the short-lived German Empire of 1848. In Hungary a whole Jewish regiment enlisted under Kossuth. Seeing that the 1848 revolutions were essentially the reaction of the rising bourgeoisie against the old feudal aristocracy and governments, it is not surprising that the Jews played so notable a part in them.

Once attention was drawn to the political and cultural life of Jewry, there was ample material on which those who disliked the Jew could draw, in order to prove that their influence could only be destructive. The Talmud remained an unknown and mysterious book for almost all non-Jews, and already in the beginning of the eighteenth century an enormous compilation of its supposedly sinister instructions had been issued by a German scholar, Eisenmenger. The fact that his scholarship was extremely faulty has never deterred those who wish to cite his authority from doing so. In the beginning of the nineteenth century several Jews, who had become converted and entered the ranks of the Roman Catholic clergy, added their quota to the denunciations of the anti-social religion of their late co-religionists. In particular the brothers Ratisbonne and the Chevalier Drach are continually quoted by antisemitic writers, and another converted Jewish priest, Father Joseph Lémann, was one of the inspirers of the antisemitism of the Dreyfus Affair.

The alarm of those who disliked the agnosticism and irreverence of the new age was still further intensified by the contemptuous attitude taken in emancipated Jewish circles towards all established traditions. Again it was in France that this feeling of outrage found its most conspicuous expression, in a work full of quotations from Jewish periodicals, speeches and books, *The Jew, Judaism, and the Judaisation of Christendom*, by Gougenot des Mousseaux, published in 1869. But society was, on the whole, too busy seeking wealth and political power for antisemitism to interest more than a small minority. The creation of political antisemitism, and the emergence of popular antisemitic movements, took place in the following decade in Germany.

In 1873 a Hamburg journalist published a small pamphlet entitled *The Victory of Judaism over Germanism*. While the signs of the victory were largely economic, Marr accepted the now popular basis of a racial difference to explain the necessity for a serious conflict with Jewish influence. For five years the pamphlet slumbered ; then a change in the German political situation brought it into prominence. In 1878 Bismarck, who had thus far been supported by the Liberal Party whose chiefs were the Jews Lasker and Bamberger, adopted a tariff policy to which the Liberals were violently opposed. As a weapon with which to beat the Liberals the prominence of their Jewish leaders was too obvious to be missed. A series of financial scandals, in some of which Jews were involved, added fuel to the flame, and in a very short time a fully developed antisemitic political programme was in the field.

From the standpoint of historical accuracy it is only from this moment onwards that the word " antisemitism " can properly be used, for it was coined in Germany about this date as a symbol that it was not the religion of the Hebrews, but the social and political activities of " Semitic " aliens in European society, that was to be attacked.

In Germany the antisemites found a leader in a Lutheran Court Chaplain, Adolf Stöcker, and for many years different antisemitic groups were sufficiently influential to secure representation in the Reichstag. Towards the end of the 'eighties a new and still more rabid antisemitic demagogue appeared in the person of Hermann Ahlwardt. He was so successful in inflaming opinion against the Jews that rioting took place in various places, and in 1891 he was even able to stage a ritual murder trial at Xanten near Düsseldorf. It ended in the dismissal of the case, but was followed by such violent agitation, to which Stöcker contributed by maintaining in the Reichstag itself the authenticity of the charge, that the accused Jew was re-arrested and retried in 1892. On this occasion the prosecuting attorney himself abandoned the trial after he had heard the flimsy and contradictory evidence on which the accusation had been based. Nevertheless, Ahlwardt continued to grow in power, and in the same year an official alliance was sealed between his party and the Conservatives.

In the following years the movement suffered a number of set-backs. Stöcker, dismissed from his post as Court Chaplain in 1885, was not re-elected to the Reichstag in 1893. In 1892 Ahlwardt was imprisoned for libel ; in 1894 the Catholics officially condemned the movement ; and in 1896 the Conservative leader, the Baron von Hammerstein, was convicted of forgery and fraud.

It is not surprising that the political power of antisemitism was unable to weather such a series of scandals. But the disease of which the political life of Germany appeared cured, had meanwhile taken root in the universities, where an intellectual antisemitic movement existed which was to prove much more dangerous. The racial ideas in the pamphlet of Wilhelm Marr can be traced to the ideas of a Frenchman, the Count de Gobineau, who in 1853 proclaimed the inequality of the human races, and the Aryan or German origin of everything which was noble and beautiful in human life and society. Gobineau wrote from a frankly political standpoint. For him the French aristocracy was the outstanding example of Germanic genius, and he opposed to it the mixed Celtic-Mediterranean scum of the bourgeoisie and proletariat, to whom power should be denied in view of their inherent and ineradicable inferiority.

In France itself the impetus of the Revolution was too strong for such ideas to make much headway, but they corresponded only too well to the national elation which followed the rise of Germany to European importance through her victories over Austria and France. Unhappily for the future, they captivated some of the most brilliant intellectual leaders in the German universities of the second half of the century. Heinrich von Treitschke, who from his Professorial Chair at Berlin dominated the whole field of German political philosophy, created the slogan of which the present government of Germany makes continual use. Identifying the "Aryans" or "Germans" not with the aristocracy but with the mass of the population, he opposed to them not a Celtic-Mediterranean stock but the Jews, and coined the phrase : "*The Jews* are our calamity." The philosopher Nietzsche, though he despised both Germans and Jews, also provided material for the antisemites, and in 1896 German racialism found its classical expression in a work of immense and perverted learning by a brilliant dilettante of English birth. *The Foundations of the Nineteenth Century*, by

Houston Stewart Chamberlain, was the bible of the antisemite until it was superseded by Hitler's *Mein Kampf*. By brilliant distortions and audacious assumptions Chamberlain claimed every effort of human society for the " Aryan " race. The proof that some great figure of the past was an " Aryan " could lie simply in the fact that other " Aryans " recognized their spiritual affinity with him. For the " Aryan " Christian no further evidence was needed that Jesus of Nazareth was an " Aryan " ; while those who rejected Christianity could, and did, by the same method proclaim Him the embodiment of the slave-mentality of the " Semites."

The " Aryan " theory has played so important a role in the evolution of modern antisemitism that it is difficult to realize that it rests on no scientific basis. The word was originally coined to describe a family of languages which obviously derived from a common stock. Thence it came loosely to be used of the peoples who employed languages of this family. Those who did so were the unwitting fathers of the next development, which was to posit a single " Aryan " race and to ascribe all virtues in civilization to its members. How vague the " Aryan " race is may be seen from the fact that those who hold the theory in France are inclined to consider that the purest Aryan type is small and dark; while German protagonists are equally convinced that it is tall and fair. In the same way each tends to locate the home of the Aryan peoples in their own territory, or at any rate not in the territory of their rivals. Every section of the map from Western Germany to Central Asia has been conclusively proved to be the home of this remarkable phantom among the peoples.

A moment's consideration of history will show that there is no necessary connexion at all between language and racial origin. The Norsemen from Scandinavia entered England in 1066 as a French-speaking people, and then learnt English from the conquered inhabitants. The Lombards and other northern tribes who settled in Italy during the "Dark Ages," as well as many Asiatics and Africans, spoke Latin, while the descendants of the Africans who inhabit Liberia to-day speak English learnt from their slave ancestors in America. On the other hand the Romans of Italy imposed their language on Celtic Gauls and Iberian Spaniards, just as the English have imposed theirs on Gaelic Scots.

Finally it would appear a little arrogant to claim that all human civilization and progress emanates from a section of the human family which includes neither the Chinese, the Egyptians, the Assyrians, nor the ancient inhabitants of Central and South America, not to speak of the " Semitic " Hebrews, Arabs and Phœnicians.

In Germany antisemitism thus played a political role for only a couple of decades, but, during this time, a pseudo-intellectual justification for it was evolved which infinitely transcended in importance the violence of Stöcker and Ahlwardt. Theories which were of German origin came to form the stock-in-trade of antisemitic activities in all other countries, and in Germany herself they increasingly dominated the conservative and ultra-patriotic sections of society and especially of the universities.

In Austria-Hungary the political movement took a somewhat different form. In Germany there had been no close alliance between the Roman Church and the antisemites, but in Austria, as in France, the attack upon the influence of the Jews found considerable support amongst those Catholics who looked with ever growing alarm on the increasing secularization of life. What in

Germany was primarily the work of Lutherans
was in Austria the work of Roman Catholics,
and even at one moment received, inad-
vertently perhaps, the direct blessing of the
Pope.

At the same time as des Mousseaux was
producing his condemnation of Judaism in
France with the support of many of the
clergy, a Roman Catholic priest, Augustus
Rohling, in the Rhineland was introducing
violent attacks on Judaism and the Jews into
the paper which he edited. But the real
activities of Rohling date from the time when
he was appointed Professor of Catholic
Theology at the University of Prague (in
those days, of course, an Austrian pro-
vincial university). In actual fact it seems
that his knowledge of Hebrew was of the
slightest, for most of the material which he
originally published under the title *The
Talmud-Jew* was taken over, and often mis-
understood, from Eisenmenger. In this
book, which first appeared in 1871 before
he left Germany, every accusation against
the Jews was repeated, and Rohling to the
very end of his life declared himself a firm
believer in the existence of ritual murder.

In 1882 he stated his readiness to make a
solemn declaration on oath that Jews were

bound to work for the destruction of non-Jews, and at the same time he repeated that he had proof of the practice of ritual murder. In the following year, Rohling and his political associates, especially in Hungary, were able to give a practical turn to this accusation, and to found upon it a political movement. In the village of Tisza Eszlar a girl disappeared. In a violent speech in the Hungarian Parliament, one of the anti-semitic leaders accused the Jews of her murder, and the government of shameful complicity in that they refused to proceed against them. A number of members of the local community, including Joseph Scharf, the sexton, who was accused of playing the leading part in the crime, were thereupon arrested, tried,—and unanimously acquitted.

After this fiasco antisemitism died down in Hungary; but it had meanwhile taken root in the Austrian portion of the Dual Monarchy where it pursued a course somewhat similar to that in Germany, except that Catholics played the part played by Protestants in the latter country. As a result of various extraneous circumstances and the general complications of Austrian politics, the party reached its highest point when it received a special Papal benediction in 1895.

Though the Pope had no intention of blessing antisemitism, and said so as soon as the unfortunate implications of his act were made clear, the harm was done, and with the supposed support of the Pope the antisemites were able to conquer Vienna. The result was the election in October 1895 of Dr. Karl Lueger as Mayor, and the creation of the Viennese regime with which Hitler became familiar in adolescence, and which converted him to antisemitism. For though Lueger was at first rejected by the Emperor, he was re-elected immediately, and in March 1896 was allowed to rule through a nominee, until on his fourth re-election in March 1897 the Emperor gave way and he became Mayor.

References have already been made to the presence of antisemitic groups in France all through the nineteenth century, and to the terrible manifestation of hatred with which the century closed. The Dreyfus Affair, however, had immediate roots in the growth of a political party similar to those of Germany and Austria. As in those countries, hostility towards the Jews was largely hostility towards the whole trend of nineteenth-century development of which the Jews were taken as the classical example. Members of the old aristocracy and of the church felt alike the menace of the increasing secularism of the Republican Government and the rapidly growing materialism of social life. The chief of the movement was Edouard Drumont, a journalist with a remarkably facile and venomous pen. The Jews were by no means the only target of his attacks and many of the campaigns which he waged against the abuses of his day were thoroughly admirable. But then as now the Jews, as an identifiable minority, formed the easiest scapegoat with which to arouse popular feeling, and Drumont copied Toussenel, except that he did not warn his reader in advance that for him the word " Jew " covered large sections of society who had not submitted to the ritual of the Abrahamic Covenant. In a work of immense length, immense learning and quite stupendous inaccuracy Drumont discovered a Jew in everything which he disliked. *La France Juive* went through edition after edition. Tens of thousands of copies poured monthly from the press in the end of the 'eighties and the beginning of the 'nineties, and it aroused an enormous controversy. With this book, and the newspaper *Free Speech* (*La Libre Parole*) which he founded in 1892, an intense political campaign was undertaken.

His supposed revelations were aided by the fact that an immense political-financial scandal was at that time seriously affecting French credit, and that three prominent Jews were among the speculators involved. This scandal involved the Company responsible for the construction of the Panama Canal which went bankrupt in 1889 revealing so amazing an amount of extravagance and corruption that the winding up of its affairs lasted until 1894.

While Drumont kept the public interested by his scandals, another antisemitic leader, the Marquis de Morès roused the young aristocrats of the army to a fury of Jew-baiting. The setting of the Dreyfus Affair was largely the work of these two men and their followers.

So far it has been a question of the growth of antisemitism in the countries of Western Europe in which the Jews were wholly or partially emancipated, and in which they were almost wholly modernized. But similar feelings were giving rise to similar movements, largely inspired by German ideas, in the countries of Eastern Europe and Turkey in which the Jews were still living under medieval conditions.

In 1840 there was a dramatic accusation

of ritual murder in Damascus, which led to the deaths under torture of a number of the leaders of the Jewish community, and in which the Europeans of Damascus, especially the French, were involved. Ritual murder was an accusation previously rare outside Western Europe and Poland, but the Damascus affair was followed in the second half of the century by a whole epidemic of such accusations in Russia and the Balkan countries still under Turkish rule.

In the latter countries the Jewish population was relatively small. The bulk of the Jews of Eastern Europe lived under Russian or Rumanian rule. The situation in Russia will be discussed in the next chapter ; that in Rumania merits a certain attention, since it was the cause of the first official attempt at mediation, on the part of powers whose Jewish population was granted equality, to secure similar rights for a Jewish community which was denied it.

The Rumanian principalities were only united in 1859. Conditions were still largely medieval, and the Jews served as middle-men and agents of the nobles. The native middle class was very small, and the peasantry were easy-going and easily exploited by both the nobles and their agents. Citizenship was confined to Christians, whereby the Jews were excluded without being mentioned. In 1878 the Congress of Berlin, which met to settle the Eastern Question, made the recognition of Rumania conditional on the grant of citizenship and access to political rights to all residents independent of religious belief. This was easy to do in Berlin, but it was not easily accepted in Rumania, where the Jews were intensely unpopular, being forced to exploit the peasantry in the interests of the nobility, and holding the peasants also in their power as shopkeepers and moneylenders.

The western powers attempted to insist on their point of view, but all that Rumania finally conceded to their protest was to pass an act allowing for the naturalization of individuals by separate acts of parliament. The result was that the immense majority of Rumanian Jews were still " resident aliens " at the end of the war of 1914–18. In the interval there had been serious unrest culminating in a rising against the Jews and the landowners in 1907 which required over 100,000 soldiers to suppress.

While the nineteenth century passed quietly for the Jewish communities of England, Holland, and Italy, none of which were particularly large, yet the extent of the hostility which Jews encountered on their entry into European society inevitably exercised a profound effect upon them. After a few initial hesitations they had entered this new world with an immense enthusiasm, and with a passionate desire to forget the past. They had assimilated themselves as rapidly as they could to the ways of life of the majority. Numbers of the wealthier and more cultured had carried their reaction against the ghetto, and everything for which it stood, to the point of asking for baptism into the religion of the majority. Others had undergone the same formality in order still further to hasten, not their acceptance by society, but their admission to the professions and the circles still closed to them.

With the enthusiasm of converts they inevitably became " plus catholique que le Pape " and attempted to still whatever murmur of discontent their appearance caused by the passionate protestation of their loyalty. Yet it was not wholly an unworthy motive which led them into the tragic position of denying their own inheritance, rich as it was in heroism and endurance. The fields which were opened to them by access to the culture and science of the modern world were fields entrancing to the keen intelligences of Israel, starved for so long on the tattered relics of what had once been an intellectual life richer and more varied than that of their Christian contemporaries. They had at least four centuries to catch up—and they caught up, to outward appearances, in a single generation.

But the change was too rapid for mental or spiritual health, especially when it encountered a rising tide of hostility. The strain imposed was terrific and many bent under it. Jewish life became restless and feverish ; mental disorders were more frequent than among the rest of the population ; the suicide rate was higher ; Jews plunged into every new movement of political and artistic fashion, seeking ever the acceptance which society was not wholly prepared to surrender them. Some, of course, settled down into their environment without difficulty ; many remained loyal to their own old traditions in spite of the temptations of the new life around them. But everywhere rents appeared in the antique fabric of the communities. If desire for innovation met with an intransigence of orthodoxy, longings to be merged in the general body-politic were answered by the emergence of Jewish nationalism.

The victory could lie with neither side.

Individuals might pass into the general society, but their children, if not themselves, were lost to the Jewish communities ; those who remained loyal could not but maintain a separation which they regretted, partly because there were customs they did not wish to abandon, partly because there were co-religionists still struggling for the freedom they had themselves obtained. To their honour the citizens of the Mosaic religion of Western Europe refused to abandon the unemancipated Jews of the rest of the continent. In political and educational organisations they worked continually for their improvement, and thereby allowed themselves to become a target for antisemitic attacks.

Sir Moses Montefiore and Adolphe Crémieux identified themselves with the Jews of Damascus throughout the stress of the ritual murder accusation of 1840. The former journeyed continually into Eastern Europe, Russia, Syria and Palestine on behalf of his less happy brethren, and the latter was the first President of the " Universal Israelite Alliance," whose main aim was to uplift the condition of the Jews still living in degradation in the countries of the Near East.

So the tides of evolution swung to and fro

until more than three-quarters of a century
had passed since emancipation first began.
Then, just as the main dangers seemed over,
political antisemitism sprang suddenly into
the arena of party politics in Germany in
1878; but three years later an immense
catastrophe befell the Jews of Eastern Europe,
which was ultimately to arouse everywhere
a hostility which has not yet died down. In
the spring of 1881 began the pogroms in
Russia which were to lead to the upheaval
and replanting of nearly a quarter of the
Jewish population of the world in less than
two generations.

# CHAPTER IV

## THE RUSSIAN CATASTROPHE

THE Jews had originally come into Europe
from the south-west, following the western
trade routes of the Roman world. The
Crusades, from the end of the eleventh
century onward, had led to a steady movement in a north-easterly direction, out of
the line of march of the crusading armies.
As the Middle Ages progressed Western
Europe largely emptied itself of Jews, and
their numbers tended steadily to increase
along its eastern frontiers. There Holy
Russia imposed a barrier against further
penetration by refusing admission to such
unbelievers within her frontiers. The wave
of flight was piled up against that barrier,
and led to an extensive settlement within
the wide boundaries of the ancient kingdom
of Poland, where Jews formed a most useful
section of the body-politic, serving as a
middle class between feudal lord and ignorant
peasantry.

During the same centuries another wave

had been spreading slowly across the Black Sea, through the Crimea and into the territories which now form south-western Russia. The ethnic origin of these Jews was, to a large extent, not Semitic but Hittite and Tartar ; and it is among them that is found most frequently those Jewish features which the antisemitic press loves to caricature. And the irony of it is that these " Hittite " features might by modern " racial " nomenclature be called the most " Aryan " characteristic of the Jew, for the language of the Hittites is now believed to belong mainly to the " Aryan " family of languages.

If one aspect of Russian policy was the exclusion of Jews from permanent settlement within her territory, another aspect was her imperialist ambition. The two came into conflict when her steady spread towards the south and west in the eighteenth and nineteenth centuries brought within her empire an enormous population of unwanted Jews. At the end of the eighteenth century she unscrupulously divided Poland with Prussia and Austria, and the lion's share fell to her—including the lion's share of Poland's Jewish inhabitants ; during the same period she acquired the Crimea ; in

1812 she collected Bessarabia; and, at the downfall of Napoleon, she added the Grand Duchy of Warsaw. In all these provinces there were numerous Jews. Her imperialism had thus brought beneath her sovereignty a Jewish population amounting to several millions.

Down to the end of Tsardom she remained determined to exclude this unwanted mass from penetration into the old provinces of Russia. A new kind of ghetto was created in the form of a series of provinces along the western frontier in which the Jews were compelled to live, and even within these provinces their rights of settlement and choice of occupation were severely restricted. Outside of these provinces selected categories of Jews might reside, visit certain fairs, and, provided they did not exceed a small proportion of the total enrolment, study at the universities. The area of settlement was known as the Pale, and it contained more than a half of the Jewish population of the world.

The Jews who thus passed under Russian domination were among the poorest and most downtrodden of this people. No breath of reform or of modern life and culture had touched them in the primitive towns and villages where they dwelt. Miserably poor themselves, it was their unhappy function in the corrupt feudalism of their surroundings to reduce to still further poverty the ignorant and oppressed peasantry amongst whom they lived. For a very large percentage of the Jewish population was occupied with the preparation and sale of alcohol, which was a manorial monopoly almost universally farmed out to Jews. But while this unhappy occupation neither raised their status nor endeared them to the population who lived perpetually indebted to the innkeepers, it must not be overlooked that they also performed valuable functions in the sale of agricultural commodities and the provision to the peasant of such instruments and personal effects as he needed to buy.

The policy of Russia was still further to degrade the Jews by continuous oppressive legislation, and, at the same time, to hold out the offer of complete liberation from oppression to those who would accept the faith of the Orthodox Church. Down to 1864 converts actually received a financial reward as well as the removal of all disabilities. The laws were brutal in the extreme, and the general principle that everything was forbidden which was not expressly permitted opened the door to continual bribery and corruption on one side and to equally continual pettyfogging oppression on the part of local officials on the other. Jews paid double the taxes of the corresponding sections of the non-Jewish community ; their communal autonomy was continually whittled down and disregarded, except when it was made the instrument of specially hateful regulations.

Of these none was more horrible than the edict of Nicholas I of 1827 which regulated military service. In spite of the fact that the Jews possessed none of the privileges of citizenship, they were compelled to undertake a double share in military service, and the selected number of conscripts for any year could be taken from any males between the ages of twelve and twenty-five. At times even boys of eight and nine were seized to be turned into soldiers. This was brutal enough, but it was not the worst. The children were taken to the very opposite ends of Russia for their service, which lasted twenty-five years counting from the age of eighteen. In the filthy barracks in which they were herded together the non-commissioned officers combined the duties of instructor with that of missionary, and every effort was made to compel these unhappy children, far from their parents and every Jewish influence, to abjure their faith. Their food was deliberately confined to pork for periods which compelled them to eat it or to die of starvation. They were ordered to perform some Christian act, and scourged until they were dead or unconscious if they refused. They were brought to the font on parade, where refusal to obey the order to enter the water was a military act of disobedience visited with the most terrible punishments; and at the end of their twenty-five years service, those few—for it was painfully few— who survived and retained their loyalty to Judaism, were immediately expelled from the city where their service had been performed, and ignominiously returned to the Pale. Only in 1856 were the worst brutalities of this system abandoned, but to the very end of the imperial regime the barbarity of military service was one of the worst terrors confronting Russian Jewish youth.

In the middle of the century there came to the throne one from whom much was expected. Alexander II was a man of very different type from Nicholas I and there is no doubt of the excellence of his intentions. But the effort involved in the emancipation of the serfs exhausted both the emperor and the bureaucracy ; and, though some of the worst of the laws of the period were modified or abandoned, no fundamental change was made in the treatment of the Jews. When a reaction set in a decade before his assassination in 1881, enough remained of the previous tradition to make life a burden and a misery for the bulk of the Jewish population.

This was the easier in that what amelioration there had been had never touched the mass of this population. It had taken the form of improving the lot of selected individuals and classes. Wealthy merchants and university graduates were allowed to reside outside the Pale. Artisans who were members of gilds might seek work wherever they liked—but the moment they were found unemployed they were sent straight back to the Pale. For the rest conditions were made increasingly rigorous. Reforms, when they were made, were dropped before they had a chance of proving their effects, and those who were affected by them were then pronounced intractable and unteachable. An agricultural scheme was proposed, for example, in Siberia, and when large numbers of Jews were actually on their way there the scheme was suddenly abandoned, and the

Jews concerned treated as wandering vagrants, to be arrested and sent elsewhere at the will of the government.

Even in the misery in which they lived the Jews were given no security. They were continually in danger of being hounded from one refuge to another. In a moment of zeal the government would decide that the famines which continually smote the western provinces, and which were due to the selfishness and indifference of the landlords, were due to the impoverishment of the peasants by the Jews. All the rural Jewish inhabitants of the Pale would therefore be suddenly sent into the already overcrowded towns—a measure which was the easier in that the Jews all had to register as town-dwellers. Then it was decided that this or that town possessed privileges which were incompatible with Jewish residence, and thousands of Jews would be uprooted to establish themselves as best they might elsewhere. These unintentional refugees could never regain security, for, expelled from the township or province of their birth, they had lost their registration, and might at any time be moved on again at the simple whim of an official. As with military service bribery was the only weapon with which a

Jew could purchase any basis for his existence, and the maw of the official class was insatiable.

It was not only in relation to Jews that the second half of the reign of Alexander II marks a reaction. From that time until the revolution of 1917 the government was more and more completely estranged from the general population, and particularly from the intellectuals. Revolutionary projects of varying intensity possessed the minds of almost all the professional classes. The assassins and organizers of assassins, who were responsible for hundreds of political murders during the next half-century, were mostly students or men and women of education. It was a student of nineteen who threw the first bomb at Alexander II on March 13, 1881, and the girl who waved her handkerchief as a signal of his approach was the Countess Sophie Perowska.

After the assassination of the Tsar the bureaucracy and the landed aristocracy took fright. They became the resolute opponents of all concessions to liberal or constitutional demands, and in this they were supported by the temperaments of his two successors. Neither Alexander III nor Nicholas II understood, or desired to understand, the new sentiments which were stirring in the minds of their people. Both were honestly convinced that to their exceedingly limited intelligences—for neither of them were men of any brilliance—was entrusted the power of deciding what was best for an empire of over a hundred million souls. And from 1880 to 1905 there stood behind the Czars Constantine Petrovich Pobêdonostsev, Procurator of the Holy Synod, brilliant, ruthless, the inveterate enemy of progress in any form, the advocate and architect of an ecclesiastical police state which was only shattered by the war and the revolution.

There were, of course, changes and apparent advances towards constitutionalism during this period, but they were always too late and inadequate. They satisfied neither peasant nor intellectual. In such conditions universal discontent was as inevitable as was universal corruption in a system where there was neither public control nor official responsibility. But in such conditions it was also necessary to find an outlet for popular feelings and a scapegoat who could divert attention from the fundamental weakness of the whole structure of society and the increasing ineffectiveness of the government.

Such a scapegoat was found in the Jews. Among the actual murderers of Alexander there were no Jews, but it sufficed that a Jewess kept the house in which the conspirators met. The whole responsibility was deliberately placed on their shoulders. Rumours were circulated, and there is no doubt that they originated in government circles, that the people meditated some fearful act of revenge for this " Jewish " crime. Lest they should not be clear enough about what they were meditating, the peasants were told in many cases that it was the imperial will that at Easter they should punish the Jews for their enormities.

As a result of this incitement the peasants, seeing also the advantages of loot, joined with the city rabbles in violent attacks upon the Jews which came to bear universally the ill-sounding name of *pogroms* (literally *destruction*). The facts that such attacks broke out almost simultaneously in many cities, and that the routine of the police was the same in every case, are sufficient evidence that there was nothing spontaneous about them. It was rarely until the third day that police or military interfered to stop the riots. As soon as they acted they had no difficulty in restoring order, a fair proof that they could also have prevented the disorder had they willed it.

After a fortnight of rioting and disorder
in all the districts where Jews dwelt, the
government announced that the pogroms
had been incited by the revolutionary parties,
and that this incitement had only been effective because of the natural revulsion of the
Christian population against the abominable
behaviour of the Jews. After a few months
of calm, the mob, convinced that the government had no violent objection to seeing the
Jews attacked, began again. The " summer
pogroms " spread to many cities spared at
Easter. In a number of places, where there
was no rioting, the Jewish quarters were set
on fire ; and at the end of 1881 the western
world was shocked by a new pogrom in
Warsaw, the city which had the closest
economic ties with the west, and where it
was therefore least possible to hide the facts.

To confirm the official view that the Jews
were solely responsible for the pogroms,
sixteen commissions were established in the
autumn of 1881 to inquire into the matter ;
but, although the membership of the commissions was largely made up of the classes
who had participated in the looting or
sympathized with the looters (that is the
peasants and landowners), five of them, when
actually confronted with the task of putting

on paper their views, had the courage to point out that the artificial conditions of Jewish life in Russia, and their unhealthy restriction to the Pale of Settlement, were the real reasons for their injurious economic activities.

The only action taken by the government as the result of this year of tragedy for its five million Jewish subjects was to authorize the publication of the statement that "the western frontier of Russia was open." Already in 1881 there had been over 8,000 emigrants to the United States. In the following year the number was more than doubled. For the government followed up its announcement by doing all in its power to make its meaning clear.

In March 1882 pogroms began again, and in May were published some "temporary rules" which remained in force until the war of 1914. Under these rules the Jews were not allowed to make "new" settlements in rural areas, or to buy real property or goods outside the towns. In addition they were not allowed to work on Christian festivals or on Sundays, so that their working days were considerably reduced if they wished to remain loyal to Jewish feasts and Sabbaths. There were many other vexatious regulations, and all were capable of every kind of malicious interpretation. A town in which Jews had been resident for centuries was suddenly declared to be a village, and the Jews thereupon expelled. It was the habit of Jews to go from the smaller centres to the larger for the High Holidays. On their return they might be told that they were " new " settlers, and as such refused admission.

Such " interpretations " and spasmodic pogroms made the lot of the Jews bitterer year by year. After a slight lull in 1883 the figures of emigration to the United States rose to over 15,000 in 1884. For three years it remained at that figure ; then it doubled again, and before the end of the decade the average was over 30,000 a year.

The emigrants were mostly completely penniless. They waited in crowds on the western frontier of Russia and almost expected a miracle to deliver them. Organizations such as the French *Alliance Israélite Universelle* and the German *Hilfsverein der Deutschen Juden* performed prodigies of improvisation to rescue the unhappy and starving victims. Committees sprang up along the route of the flight which provided food and clothing to the travellers. But year after year the situation in Russia grew more desperate, and the figures of the emigrants grew from tens to hundreds of thousands. Many were unable to afford even the cheapest passage to America. They dropped off all along the route, and every commercial city of Western Europe received its quota of penniless and almost starving Russian Jewish refugees. Only two trickles diverged from the immense stream which flowed into the expanding centres of the world's industry. A few of the hardier were fired with the idea of resettling in Palestine, and tiny colonies of Zionists came into being. A slightly larger number settled in the Argentine, where a wealthy Bavarian Jew, the Baron de Hirsch, had acquired a large tract of land where he hoped vainly to establish hundreds of thousands of exiles in new and independent communities.

Inevitably this immense flight changed the whole face of the Jewries of the western world.

In spite of the antisemitic movements which have already been described, the small western Jewries were rapidly becoming totally assimilated to their environment. It might almost be said that apart from the existence of enough prejudice against them to keep alive the loyalties of members to the group, western Jewry would have vanished before the turn of the century. But what was possible for tens of thousands of cultured and westernized citizens of the Mosaic Faith was impossible for the hundreds of thousands of Jews from the inexhaustible ghetto of Russia.

In a couple of decades the Jewish population of the United States rose from less than a quarter of a million to more than a million ; that of England from less than a hundred thousand to nearly a quarter of a million ; while France, Holland and Germany each received between twenty and twenty-five thousand of these refugees. The new-comers were unlike any Jews whom the west had seen for centuries. The German Jews who first arrived in England in the eighteenth century had been poor, and some had not been particularly honest, but here was a sudden irruption of the fourteenth century into the nineteenth and twentieth. Totally ignorant for the most part of the elements of modern civilization, accustomed to thinking of every official as a venal enemy whose favour could at best be secured by copious bribery, compelled to live by the invention of ingenious evasions of regulations framed only for their oppression, looking on their

Gentile environment as inevitably brutal, malicious and hostile, strange in their dress, their speech, their food and their mannerisms, rigidly orthodox, they inevitably created feelings more akin to disgust than to pity, to resentment than to sympathy, in the cities of their new settlement; and this feeling was the stronger and the more inevitable for two reasons. Their own poverty compelled them to crowd into the poorest districts, where the native population was most ignorant and suspicious of "foreigners"; and their great numbers coupled with the suspicion of their neighbours intensified their clannishness and the difficulty of the simplest political, social and economic assimilation.

The Jewish communities of the west made the greatest efforts to smooth their way into normal life. Shelters were created at important centres of transit and destination; schools were opened, relief was given to the aged and infirm, work was found for the able-bodied, orphanages were created for those who had lost their parents in the pogroms, legal assistance was given to those in need of it. It was a wonderful example of solidarity, and it was solidarity of a kind which could earn only the gratitude of the receiving nations. For the voluntary work of the Jews took off the shoulders of the rest of the community much of the burden which such an immigration inevitably entails. On the other hand it was not the Jews who opened the doors to immigration : it was the epoch of the " open door," especially in England and America, where the industrial expansion of those countries required a continual flow of new workers, and made it possible for the immense majority of the immigrants to find in a relatively short time some occupation from which they could earn a meagre living. Indeed not many years passed before the most active and able of them had reached prosperity and some even wealth.

While the Jewish communities made every effort to succour their brethren in distress, it was still difficult for such large numbers really to be absorbed into their new environment. The Gentile world was handicapped by the fact that the new-comers spoke only Yiddish or Russian, and did not know even the script in which western languages were written. The Churches and settlements which abounded in industrial cities were hindered in their attempt at closer contact both by the suspicion of conversionism which was inevitable on the part of Jews, and by the fact that their own efforts were often tinged by a missionary outlook which saw in the rendering of humanitarian assistance primarily an opening for the preaching of the Christian religion.

Governments and municipal administrations were likewise handicapped by the primitive state in which social and industrial legislation then was. In any case the laws, such as they were, were not framed to deal with large groups of persons accustomed to totally different standards of living. The Jewish workers were largely working for Jewish masters, who had themselves only arrived a short while earlier. They were paid miserable wages, worked for abominably long hours, and were housed in horrible conditions. All this created indignation on the part of the Gentile workers, for the immigrants worked for a rate at which they themselves could not live; and the shop-keepers and manufacturers were likewise antagonized by the appearance of cheap goods with which they could not compete, and by the opening of shops by people prepared to accept half the usual profits. What was not realized was that these conditions were often Paradise compared with what the Russian Jews had been accustomed to in Russia, and that these practices were the result of ignorance and the acceptance of a standard long abandoned in the west, not of malice, covetousness or indifference to the welfare of the non-Jewish world.

As the end of the century approached conditions began to get a little easier ; the new-comers began to settle down. But Russia had not said her last word. In 1905 the pogroms broke out again with a new intensity, and the flood of refugees again assumed enormous proportions. Within twelve months 125,243 Jews left Russia for the United States alone.

Everything had to be begun all over again, although this time the new-comers received a good deal of help from Russian immigrants who had already found their own feet, and could now give employment and education to new arrivals.

Unhappily, before this second wave had a chance of being absorbed an event took place which accentuated the distinction between them and the rest of the population.

In 1914 war broke out, and these Russian Jews, settled in England, France, and later those in America, were called upon to fight as allies of the country which for generations had maltreated them, crushed them and driven them into exile. The horrors of military service in Russia itself was a very living memory to them; the responsibilities of democratic citizenship were something which they had still to learn and understand. While the youth of older Jewish communities volunteered or fought as conscripts with the same enthusiasm and heroism as their Gentile neighbours, it was asking too much of the new arrivals to expect them to face military service in combination with such an ally as imperial Russia herself with anything but the most intense reluctance. In the countries where conscription existed before the war many tens of thousands of Russian Jews had never taken out naturalization papers at all, not because of their expense, but because of their hatred of military service. Evasions, self-mutilations, desertions were not unknown, and though men in calm mood would easily understand and pardon such a situation, yet in the fevered temper of the war, both among the Allies and among the Central powers, complaints were loud and frequent against the disloyalty and ingratitude of "the Jews," and were not silenced by the visible fact that those Jews who had learned the meaning of citizenship and understood its responsibilities gave their lives in equal numbers with the rest of the population.

During the war immigration of the pre-war kind was impossible, but, on the other hand, the whole of the eastern front lay in the districts of Russia which had formed part of the Pale. A new type of refugee became familiar to the Central Powers, the refugee from the war area. He could only flee westward, to Germany, Austria, Hungary or Roumania, for to flee eastwards was impossible for him. During the war itself these refugees were welcomed, for they could be made to work in munition factories. But after the war, during the terrible years of starvation and depression which followed, an immense cry went up against the burden of this new " invasion."

Meanwhile, the great unwieldy empire of the Tsars was hastening to its inevitable collapse. The breath of liberalism which, in the middle of the nineteenth century, had freed the serfs had never blown again. Groups of men who began as liberals turned more and more to violent revolution as the only solution. The towns and the mines of Siberia were peopled with those who should have been at the forefront of national life, and in every capital abroad there were little groups of exiles plotting revolution.

Antisemitism was used continually as a

safety-valve for the masses, but it could not avail to conceal from either the outer world or the leaders of Russian thought the necessity for a radical transformation of the whole structure, which, by the beginning of the twentieth century, had sunk into such confusion that the ablest ministers of the Tzar could scarcely make it work.

As was to be expected, the Jewish middle classes sympathized with the reforming parties, since they had the additional reason for detesting the government that they were exposed to continual petty persecution, even when their residence outside the Pale preserved them from actual physical danger or the violent destruction of their property. Things reached such a pass that an English baronet and member of Parliament was turned out of his hotel and expelled from Moscow on the day of his arrival, on the grounds that Jews were not allowed to sleep in the ancient Muscovite capital. That a number of the younger and more hotheaded Jews, together with some of the Jewish proletariat, sided with the revolutionaries and terrorists is equally natural.

In 1917, under the strain of the war, the empire finally crashed. The Jews everywhere hailed its disappearance, and the installation of the democratic government which followed, with the uttermost joy. Unhappily the government of Kerensky was unable to hold its own, and after only a few months collapsed before the brilliant and ruthless strategy of Lenin and the Bolshevik leaders. The October revolution of 1917 installed the present government of Russia in the saddle.

There is no doubt that at the beginning the bulk of the Jews of Russia were amongst the most vigorous opponents of the Bolsheviks. In the elections for a "constituent assembly" which followed the downfall of the Tsar the Jewish districts recorded the strongest votes against the Bolsheviks. This was natural, as nothing in Jewish tradition or experience in Russia predisposed a Jew to be a "collectivist." The original strength of the Bolsheviks lay in the factory workers and Russian urban proletariat. Jews, like peasants, hated the Tsarist regime, but all that they wanted was to be their own unrestricted masters. At the same time, it very soon became clear to them, that the acceptance of the Bolshevik regime was the only possible policy, and indeed the essential basis of survival. For the armed intervention of the Allies in support of the various generals of the White armies, led to the bloodiest pogroms that had ever marked Jewish history. The victims were to be numbered in tens of thousands, and whole communities were entirely wiped out. And, by the end of 1918 there was no *via media* possible. If the Jews did not accept the Bolshevik regime, the only alternatives before them were either to be massacred by the White armies for the mere fact of being Jews, or to be shot by the Bolsheviks for being enemies of the people.

In the result their acceptance of the regime also meant a prominence which has been the basis of the continuous identification of " the Jews " with communism. In the original leadership of the party there were no Jews at all. Bolshevism may be an adaptation of the writings of Karl Marx, but it was an entirely Russian adaptation. It was less than a couple of decades before the Revolution that a number of Jews became prominent among the personalities of the Bolshevik party. The first government contained about a third of Jewish commissars (the actual figures are quite impossible to establish, but they lay between a quarter and a half). They represented little more than themselves in so far as Russian Jewry was concerned. But once the civil war broke out, and the appalling massacres of the middle and upper classes began, there disappeared into the White Armies, exile or the grave the bulk of those who had the education to fill government posts. Of those who were left the Jews showed by far the highest proportion of men who could read and write ; and since, as has already been said, they were compelled by circumstances to accept the regime, they found themselves also compelled to provide a totally disproportionate number of its clerks and officials. The ordinary public, Russian or foreign, met these second-grade officials more often than they met the actual leaders of the revolution themselves. The number of Jews among them was too great to escape comment. The ascription of the whole revolution to " the Jews " was not unnatural, however erroneous, especially as the foreign observers did not see the much larger numbers of Jews to whom the revolution, with its detestation of the petty trading class to which most Jews belonged, spelt complete ruin.

Had the frontiers been open, there would have been as large an exodus of Jews from Russia after the war as there had been in the years preceding it, but the final argument which compelled them to accept the regime was the fact that all the countries on the western frontier, once they had established order within their borders, closed them to the east, and that America and the countries of Western Europe would no longer accept immigrants. Some thousands of Jews managed, undoubtedly, to penetrate into Poland, the Baltic countries and Rumania, but they were but a fraction of the hundreds of thousands who would have liked to follow them.

# CHAPTER V

## TENSIONS AND TENDENCIES IN PRE-WAR JEWRY

WHEN the catastrophe of 1914 burst upon the world there were no social groups less prepared to meet it than the Jewries of the different countries involved. The tremendous experiences of the previous century were only half-digested ; innumerable problems of adjustment were still unsolved ; in its inner construction and in its external relationships, the Jewish world was completely disorganized. Only small groups of more or less wealthy and cultured western Jews, to whom " the wandering Jew " was little more than a legend of a past now happily—as they thought —for ever vanished, had really adjusted themselves to their environment, and even they possessed far less security than they believed.

In the religious, the social and the political fields, Jewry was rent by bitter divisions, almost as deep as those which divided them according to national loyalties in the nightmare years of war.

The Christian world has become so accustomed to religious toleration, and to the idea that religion is a private affair of the individual, that it has become difficult to conceive of the entirely different place which Judaism occupies in Jewish history. The spheres of "religious" and "secular" activities are so clearly separated in the minds of the ordinary man that he cannot readily think of a world in which the secular does not exist. Yet such a world was the ghetto of pre-emancipation Jewry. But not only was the whole life of the Jew determined in terms of his religious allegiance, but the structure of Judaism had for centuries been adapted to the twin ends of providing a centre for the whole life of the individual Jew, and of shutting out the great world of Gentile life and culture beyond the ghetto walls. The difference between Jew and Gentile was far more than that they attended different places of worship on a particular day in the week. The bearded men with side-locks, the shaven-headed married women could not but be religious Jews and Jewesses; their dress was different from that of the Gentiles; their speech was different, for few Jews knew, except for business purposes, any other languages than Yiddish and Hebrew; their laws were different, for Jewish disputes were adjusted in the ancient rabbinical courts according to Talmudical decisions, and few Jews ever brought their disputes into Gentile courts ; their food was different, and a Jew would not eat in a Gentile house ; and all these customs possessed the sanction, and were guarded by the warnings, of religion. To attack them, to modify or alter them was an assault on religion itself.

Such a position could not long survive the emancipation without serious cracks appearing in its walls. This was all the more inevitable in that centuries of repression and of an artificial existence in the little world of the ghetto had played havoc with the spirituality and profundity of true rabbinic religion. In scholarship and breadth of interest, in toleration and open-mindedness, in sincerity and purity of life, the Judaism of the tenth century had nothing to fear from a comparison with its rival Christianity ; it was rather the Church which feared contact with Judaism. But a thousand years is a long time for the spiritual vitality of any religion to endure continual repression, persecution and contempt. It is a matter for understanding pity, and neither for sneers nor blame, that traditional orthodoxy could not meet the new situation; that it would accept no compromise; that it tried to forbid access to the new fields of learning and inquiry opened to the young Jew by the emancipation; that it regarded modification of its ritual or practice with horror.

And yet those who could no longer accept unreservedly the dictates of orthodoxy did not necessarily wish wholly to abandon the religion of their fathers. They insisted that it was possible for them to remain loyal Jews without rejecting modern knowledge, or modern dress and manners; they accepted the value in the past of those rules of dress, conduct and diet which had erected a rigid wall between Jew and Gentile, but they proclaimed such barriers fallen with the walls of the ghetto. Judaism possessed profound ethical principles, principles of universal significance; it was in these that they saw a centre for their loyalty, and the rest they discarded. It is difficult for the Gentile to realize that such details as the permissibility of an organ in a synagogue could appear a fundamental on which no compromise was possible. But Judaism was a whole, and in any totalitarian system there is inevitably little difference between major and minor issues. It takes but a little hole to let all the air out of a pneumatic tyre!

Reformed types of Judaism some more some less extreme, sprang up in the middle of the century, and gained many adherents among the western Jewries of Germany and America ; in other countries, such as England and France, small reform congregations also existed. The strife between them and the orthodox synagogues was, and still is, bitter, and it was made bitterer by the fact that there is no central authority in Judaism which could seek a *via media* and win the acceptance of the large majority of the communities. In such a situation the orthodox argument was that no change could possibly be made because there was no authority to sanction it ; that of the liberals was to reply that in such a situation each congregation must assume its own responsibility for change.

The flight from Russia accentuated the struggle. Western orthodoxy, with but few exceptions, had made a number of concessions to modernism. Orthodox Jews and even rabbis were shaven ; side locks were universally abandoned ; by the compromise of not eating meat orthodox Jews accepted the hospitality of their Gentile neighbours ; and ceremony and belief had been pruned of many of the accretions of superstition with which the past had encrusted them.

The new arrivals from Russia knew no such compromises ; in the slums of western industrial cities they attempted to re-establish life as it was in the ghettoes of the Russian Pale ; the Talmud and its commentaries formed their only reading ; the synagogue and its services their only diversion. Moreover, they in turn were divided into innumerable small congregations following particular rabbis and particular schools of thought. Emancipation meant nothing to them, they accepted of the modern world only its economic freedom.

Such a life might survive amongst those who were already mature when they left Russia. The cessation of persecution and discriminatory legislation satisfied them. The idea of citizenship with its opportunities and responsibilities frightened rather than attracted them. But with the children, born in the west, it was different. Brought up in the schools of their new country under systems of compulsory education, speaking its language as their native tongue, they found their parents foreign and their parents' ways unsympathetic. The synagogue with its outlandish language and ancient superstitions left them cold. And yet reform Judaism, almost entirely a prerogative of an assimilated middle class, left them still less affected, even where they had opportunities for coming into contact with it.

And indeed reform Judaism was singularly ill-equipped to catch this rising generation. Ethical religion is too cold and formal for youth. It lacks colour and makes no appeal to their imaginations ; it is too rationalized and at the same time too sublimated. An enormous proportion of the children of orthodox Russian homes found themselves with no spiritual anchorage whatever. Some drifted into left-wing movements of all kinds and found there not only the enthusiasm which appealed to them, but also the passionate interest in social righteousness which is the deepest inheritance of the ancient rabbinic tradition. Others, especially among the more prosperous, left the community altogether, intermarried with Gentiles, and accepted formally, or sincerely, the religion of the majority.

The divisions which were so conspicuous in the religious field were soon marked in the social field also. The unbounded and unreserved enthusiasm for complete assimilation which had been the natural if unreflecting ambition of the pioneer generation of emancipation was chilled by the reaction which the Jews encountered in their new life. The ambition to be assimilated could not long remain spontaneous. It became either a conscious purpose, in spite of opposition from within or without, or it was abandoned as a betrayal and a failure. Class and origin again played a large part in deciding on which side the individual Jew should stand. It was idle to expect every child of the Russian Pale instantaneously to acquire the culture and ways of life of those who had been for centuries, or at least for generations, accustomed to modern European society. It was the upper and professional classes which proclaimed themselves in Britain and elsewhere to be citizens of the Jewish faith, and stoutly asserted that nothing but attendance—or non-attendance—at a different place of worship differentiated them from their neighbours. It was the poorer classes which set first the fact of their Jewishness and looked for a formula which reconciled it to the implications of their newly-acquired citizenship.

It might have seemed that the first class would, in a few generations, have vanished from separate existence altogether, and merged themselves entirely in their environment; and it is probable that this would have happened in all western Jewries, but for the appearance of a number of unexpected factors as the century progressed.

One of the most important checks to this disappearance arose out of the wholly praiseworthy feeling of loyalty which these Jews still felt towards their less fortunate brethren. Within the community western Jews might and did despise and deride the barbarities and crudities of the children of the ghetto. But so far as the outside world was concerned, they accepted the responsibility to be their brothers' keepers, when those brothers were in physical distress through persecution or through flight. Such a feeling was very far indeed from the imaginary solidarity of antisemitic propaganda. It implied no super-government, not even a divided loyalty. It was a practical and sincere application of the principle common to both Judaism and Christianity that we should bear one another's burdens ; and it was accepted by western Jewry at considerable sacrifice to both their pockets and their position in the community. For the western Gentile was very ready at any time to accept the westernized Jew, on condition that he dissociated himself from these unassimilable and often repulsive immigrants, and from the inhabitants of the ghettoes whence they came. Torn between the desire for such acceptance and the ancient tradition of Judaism, those who frequented and those who had abandoned the synagogue alike answered the call of tradition and not of social advantage. By innumerable acts the Jewries of England, France and Germany, of America and the New World, accepted that they should be identified with the cosmopolitan and universal world of Jewry, even if the outsider saw in it a stigma, and a bar to acceptance into the desired world of national citizenships.

A second factor was the emergence of self-conscious nationalism, which was bound to affect Jews in two ways. They were themselves inevitably influenced by it, and their minds were turned to their own "nationality." In fact the urge to think of themselves as members of a "nation" gave to many a substitute for the loyalty to the religion of the synagogue which they had abandoned. But even more, the growth of nationalism among the non-Jewish population caused the slow emergence of racial ideas, by which the alienness of the Jew came to be felt as something which neither baptism nor assimilation could even modify. And when this national self-consciousness issued in political antisemitism, it seemed to many Jews that the path to assimilation was closed. For assimilation could not permanently be a one-sided affair. A Jew could not lose himself in membership of a nation unless the majority were willing to accept him.

Even so the very diversity of Jewish life and the innumerable conflicts and tensions within each community made the birth of Jewish nationalism a slow and difficult process. It is typical of the situation in the nineteenth century that in no country did a Jewish Party come into existence. Even in Galicia with its hundreds of thousands of Jews, Jewish members of the Galician diet belonged to the Polish Club. There was no platform which united the Jews of any one nation in a common political programme. From time to time issues emerged on which the immense majority of Jews were united but, the issue faced, the unity disappeared with astonishing rapidity. Clerical parties, agrarian parties, workers' parties, were common features of the democracies of almost every country. But of Jewish parties there were none.

Nor could one come into existence on the negative programme of fighting anti-semitism. That might be, indeed was, a communal responsibility for the authorities of the Jewries, but it was not a political programme. Jews were to be found in all parties as individuals, but though some parties might have more and some fewer, no party was exclusively Jewish in membership or policy. Even in parties where anti-semitic feeling was most to be found, individual Jews were also present. For it can be said of western Jewry all through the nineteenth century that it refused to abandon the idea of total emancipation with its corollary of total assimilation, in spite of all checks. After all, the special privileges which loyalty to Judaism demanded were no greater than those demanded by and conceded to Catholics or Quakers. Victory was but a matter of time.

Eastern Jewry, and the immigrants from the East, were less convinced. They saw that half of the Jewish people still lived under medieval conditions, without security, without the possibility of forgetting that a Jew was a Jew and not a Christian. They had never tasted to the full the liberty of complete acceptance, and they resigned themselves to exclusion from it with the less reluctance. It was in such soil that Jewish nationalism was ultimately firmly established, and the Zionist Movement came to birth.

It was the tragedy of the Jews that nationalism, which was a natural product of the century, and a normal development of the extension of the franchise, implied in the Jewish world a bitter assault upon all that that century had brought to them. The grant of the effective expression of citizenship to the poorer classes in England, France or elsewhere implied no conflict of loyalties ; the same grant to minorities which were not yet free, such as the Czechs or Poles, implied indeed a struggle for freedom, but one to which they could devote themselves with single-minded intensity. But to the Jew seemed to be presented two mutually exclusive alternatives. Jewish nationalism turned its back on the victories of emancipation, in that it emphatically rejected the ambition which the Jews of the west, and more prosperous Jews of the east, had set themselves, to be English, French, Russian citizens of the Jewish faith.

The history of Zionism is not to be understood simply in terms of geography or of colonization. There is no question of the reality of the devotion to the actual city of Jerusalem in the heart of historic Judaism ; nor is there any question of the fact that all through Jewish history there has been a trickle, small but steady, of Jews from all over the world back to that ancient home. But the devotion to Jerusalem has been mystical even more than geographical; the return has been made that the immigrant might be buried in the sacred soil, not that he might colonize it. The Palestinian Jews were in no sense an autonomous nation, scarcely even a political community; they lived in dire poverty on the alms of the Jews of the Dispersion, and died as representatives, not of a Jewish state, but of a scattered religious people.

The presence of these Jews in Palestine was a symbol to the Dispersion, a dramatic presentation of an age-old dream; so also was the phrase repeated at the Feast of the Passover: "Next year in Jerusalem." The phrase was not hypocritical, nor unreal, but its meaning was symbolic not geographical. Jerusalem stood as a symbol of liberty, of the removal of oppression, of an end to persecution, of equality among equals.

Had the desire for independent nationhood been a vivid reality in Jewish history, there were several occasions on which it might have been realized; Jews might have joined as a people in the great wave of colonization which spread from Europe to the rest of the world from the sixteenth century to the nineteenth. In many parts of the world they might have found a home, in some they were offered it. Both Jews and Christians formed projects for Jewish national settlement ; even Palestine stood open to them on different occasions, had they but had the general will to avail themselves of it. It is significant that the first efforts to turn even the mendicant Jews living in Jerusalem into self-supporting colonists came from non-Jewish initiative, and was a failure because Jews themselves did not support the idea. It is this background which has divided Jews into violently hostile camps on the issue of Zionism.

At the same time, the growth of such a political nationalism in the nineteenth century was neither artificial nor unworthy. Its roots were real. In the first place there was the very feeling of which mention has been already made. It may legitimately be said that there was no inherent reason why, at the touch of some new impulse, the real geographical longing for Jerusalem, hitherto faint though it was, should not take its place as an equal beside the older mystical interpretation. In the second place the very fact of emancipation placed the Jews in the middle of the stream of nineteenth century developments, and they could not remain unaffected by the enthusiasms of the new nationalisms which surrounded them. The enormous flood of Jewish histories which poured out between 1850 and 1900 revealed not only the intimate link between the history of the Jews and the histories of the countries where they dwelt, but they also emphasized the common thread running all through Jewish history whatever its geographical, economic or political diversity. Graetz and other general Jewish historians showed that Jewish history could be considered the history of a single people ; even the innumerable histories of local communities showed that there was some common factor which had always ensured survival and preserved distinctness.

When in the second half of the century, first Germany, then Russia, then France offered to the eyes of the blindest Jew the fact that emancipation had certainly not yet completed its work in the west while it had not yet begun it in the east, the emergence of a conscious Jewish nationalism was to be expected. Such a movement had to have a geographical centre. When a deliberate decision had to be taken as to where that centre should be tradition could only give one answer: Jewish nationalism must mean the return of the Jews to Palestine.

It was natural that the movement, once it came into existence, should make the strongest appeal to those who were most conscious of the misery of their lot. Nevertheless the foundation of an actual international organization was the work of an Austrian journalist whose whole attitude was changed from an ardent desire for assimilation by the experience of watching the crowds in Paris, moved to frenzy by the emotions of the Dreyfus case, howling " Down with the Jews," " Kill the Jews " around the Law Courts where one of the many trials connected with the case was being heard. If even in France, a hundred years after the revolution, such feelings were possible then it seemed to Theodor Herzl certain that there was no security for the Jews except in a land of their own.

The persecution in Russia had already brought into existence local groups of enthusiasts, and a few colonies had already been established in Palestine, where they survived through the generous help of the Baron Edmond de Rothschild. Now in 1897 Herzl was able to gather in Basel 204 delegates from all over Europe, and in successive congresses the actual programme of contemporary Zionism was elaborated.

Propaganda groups were formed in every

possible centre of Jewish settlement ; bands of young men and women trained themselves for the hard work of agricultural pioneering ; but before 1914 no striking results were obtained. The immense majority of wealthy Jews, being essentially the very groups who were most completely satisfied with things as they were, refused their financial support to the scheme. Herzl lacked the money to be able to exercise decisive influence on the Sultan and to secure a proper guarantee either for the stability of his proposed settlements, or for conditions which would favour their free development. The greatest Jewish philanthropist of the period, the Baron de Hirsch, who spent an immense fortune on attempting to ameliorate the conditions of the distressed Jews of Russia, and who bequeathed £2,000,000 for the same purpose, refused to assist the Zionist scheme of colonizing Palestine. At a moment when concentrated effort was particularly necessary, the Baron set his heart on, and gave all his money for, colonization schemes in Latin America. Yet, in spite of this, the Zionist Movement could claim in 1914 to have settled 12,000 Jews in 59 colonies in Palestine, of whom the immense majority came from Eastern Europe. But they could not yet claim that either economically or politically their adventure had achieved real stability.

The overwhelming majority of the Jewish population of the world were compelled to look for a solution of their problem, not in Palestine, but in the countries of their residence. Numbers alone made any hope of settling an important proportion of the people in Palestine in any conceivable future fantastic. While exact figures are impossible, the Jewish population in 1912 was estimated at about eleven and a half millions. Of these nearly half, over five millions, still lived in Russia, in spite of the fact that the Jewish population of the United States had leapt from about fifty thousand in 1850 to nearly two million in 1910, and that the new-comers were almost all of Russian origin. Austria-Hungary had a Jewish population of over two millions, of whom nearly a million lived in what is now Southern Poland. In all the rest of Europe there were only about a million and a half Jews, and of these again, a considerable proportion were Russian refugees.

While the numbers and dispersion of the population provided a numerical and geographical obstacle to resettlement in Palestine, the economic obstacle was even more striking.

The primary need of Palestine was for agricultural pioneers. But the Jews had been made by history almost universally into town-dwellers, and by modern history into dwellers in the great industrial cities and the capitals of the modern world. One sixth of the entire Jewish population lived in the six cities of New York, Warsaw, Budapest, Odessa, London and Vienna. In these cities the great majority of the Jewish population belonged to that urban proletariat which is most incapable of being uprooted and planted on the land. Petty artisans and shopkeepers, they had neither the physique nor the outlook out of which pioneers can be made. Moreover, the whole trend of the age was against agricultural settlement. Everywhere there was a drift from the country to the town, a drift which is still with us. In such circumstances the fact that the Zionist and other organizations had succeeded in turning some hundreds of thousands of Jews into successful farmers of one kind and another was no mean achievement. It touched but the fringe of the problem, but at least it showed that, given the right circumstances, the Jews were as capable of following all the normal occupations of an independent community as were any other people.

The final obstacle has already been mentioned : the tragic fact that Zionism ran counter to the whole ambition of nineteenth-century Jewry to accept with open arms the opportunities which were offered by emancipation. In the wealthy communities of the west it was only among the poor and the newly arrived that it flourished, and even among those it met with the fiercest opposition from the more orthodox section of the population, to whom it was little less than sacrilege to attempt to achieve by political negotiation that which was promised as a final expression of divine favour, and was to be achieved by miraculous means.

If the assimilated communities were the main opponents of Zionism yet it was from the condition of just these Jewries that the Zionists drew one of the main arguments for the historic necessity of their movement. The trend of events gave some justification to their contention that, unless Jewish nationalism became a reality, the separate existence of the Jews would shortly vanish.

It was certainly true that the breaking down of the walls of the ghetto had broken down many other barriers also. The rate of intermarriage and the rate of baptism both increased steadily during the nineteenth century. While the efforts of missionaries met with but little response, the argument of social advantage had a compelling influence on many who were already Jews only in name. The children of mixed marriages were rarely brought up in the Jewish faith, and their children in turn were often completely unconscious of the inheritance of Jewish blood. The agony of the " non-Aryans " in modern Germany shows both the number of such marriages, and the rapidity with which the Jewish origin of an ancestor was forgotten. And even those who remained " Jews " were less and less able to explain wherein their " Jewishness " consisted. They followed no traditional observances, they were often totally ignorant of Jewish history and custom. They were " Jews " only because the antisemites said they were. But on such a basis there was neither probability nor, indeed, reason for their survival as a separate unit among the peoples of the world.

Such was the situation of Jewry when the world war broke out in 1914 and presented it with innumerable new problems, and, at its end, appeared to open unbelievable new possibilities.

# PART II
# THE POST-WAR WORLD

JEWISH PROBLEM IN THE MODERN WORLD
number in the western Jewries in 1914 were
very recent immigrants from Russia, who
were not citizens, and had little knowledge
of what it was they were expected to fight
for except that they were caught on the side
of their land against that of Russia
of Russia.

## CHAPTER VI

### THE WAR AND THE PEACE CONFERENCE

IT was said in the last chapter that no
group was less prepared to meet the crisis
of 1914 than the Jews. It is also true that
there was no group more tragically affected
by the war. In the first place it was inevitable in a community whose members were
scattered in every country, that family relationships should have continually cut across
political frontiers. Cousins fought against
cousins in the different armies ; even brothers
against brothers, fathers against children.
This needs to be remembered when the
charge is heard that the Jews were unreliable
during the war. As a matter of cold statis-
tics cases where such relationships really
affected political loyalties must have been
very few, for the proportion of Jews engaged
in the British, French, German and other
armies was as high as the proportion of the
Jewish communities to the general population. This proportion is all the more remarkable when it is realized what a large

number in the western Jewries in 1914 were very recent immigrants from Russia, who were not citizens, and had little knowledge of what it was they were expected to fight for except that they were to fight on the side of their hated enemy, the Tsarist Government of Russia.

On the eastern battle-front it was difficult for Jews to decide what attitude they were to take. The whole zone was seething with movements for freedom among the subject peoples of the Tsar and the Austrian Emperor ; and the former group were as naturally encouraged by the German armies as the latter were by the Allies. If the Jews sided with these movements, what would be their fate if Russia or Austria won ? What would happen to their husbands, sons and brothers, conscripts in the Russian and Austrian armies ? What better treatment could they expect from the non-Jewish population if the subject peoples achieved their freedom ? The Pole, the Rumanian, the Czech, the Lithuanian, who was plotting treason against his political sovereign, the Tsar or the Emperor of Austria, knew exactly for what he was committing treason ; it was for his own freedom. The Jew was only asked to exchange one master for another, and whichever he chose, the other, if he won, might exact terrible vengeance from him. It is an old human tendency to prefer the devil we know to the devil we know not. But in the result the unexpected happened. Both Russia and Austria collapsed ; and the succession states of both empires started life with the conviction that their new Jewish subjects were not reliable. This was particularly the tragic lot of the more than three million Jews who inhabited the new Poland, some of whom had been active on the Russian side, both during the Great War and in the conflict of the new Polish state with the Bolshevik Government. Fighting with her back to the wall Poland forgot the Jews who were taking her part as they had at many periods of her history, and remembered only the few who then sided against her—on both sides the normal weaknesses of human nature.

If the subject peoples of Eastern and Central Europe looked to the issue of the war for a new regulation of their status, and if the same was true of the Jews in those regions, Jews in the west desired no alteration of their position. The national Rolls of Honour united Jew and non-Jew as they had never been joined before. It was a natural hope that the brotherhood born in the trenches would finally dissolve the old poisons of antisemitism from the body-politic of democratic countries. All that western Jews were anxious to do was to obtain the same felicity for their still un-emancipated brethren.

For them the crucial year was 1917. On April 4 of that year the first Russian Revolution, by a single act, emancipated several million Jews ; in November came the " Balfour Declaration " by which the British Government declared its approval of the establishment in Palestine of a national Jewish home, a declaration which was con-firmed by the other Allied Governments.

These two events completely changed the world Jewish situation, and when President Wilson in his fourteen points issued on January 8, 1918 emphasized the rights of small nations as a basic principle of the coming peace, the question of the position of the Jewish populations of the potential new countries immediately rose in the minds of Jewish leaders. Two parties were formed, which roughly represented the western-assi-milated, and the eastern-nationalist points of view. English Jewry, represented by the *Board of Deputies of British Jews*, was mainly interested in the removal of all personal disabilities, and in guarantees that every individual Jew in the new states should be able fully to enjoy such liberty as was enjoyed by the rest of the population. The other party wished to secure recognition for the Jewish communities as separate cultural and political entities. While it was geographically impossible that a Jewish state should be formed anywhere in Europe, it was but just that those new rights which would be won by Poles, Czechs or others through the fact that they became members of a sovereign state of their own nationality, should also be accorded to the large Jewish populations which these states would discover within their frontiers. The problem was not wholly a Jewish one for, however the frontiers were drawn, there were bound to be several million other Europeans living under the rule of majorities to which they did not themselves belong.

When finally the delegates of the Allied Powers met at Versailles to redraw the map of Europe, the Jews were by no means the only group seeking a form of recognition of the same moral order as the concession of national states to national homogeneous populations. But, while not the only group interested in minority rights, Jews took a leading position in the discussions, since they alone constituted minorities in all the countries under consideration. The result, for both Jews and the others, was the drafting of a series of Minority Treaties which guaranteed the free exercise of cultural rights to minorities, while assuring them at the same time of perfect equality before the law with all other citizens.

These treaties found no favour with the countries which were requested to sign them. In the first place, filled as they were with the vanity of new sovereignties, they saw in this demand that they should guarantee to treat certain of their citizens in particular ways, an affront to their national dignities, and a suggestion that they were less civilized than the countries imposing these conditions. Poland registered the very strongest protest, and yielded only to personal pressure from Clemenceau, and Rumania went so far as to withdraw from the conference altogether, and was only brought back by a formal ultimatum from the Principal Allied Powers.

While the Minority Treaties have proved a failure, yet it is easy to see both how reasonable and how necessary they appeared in those days. The minorities concerned differed from the majorities in language and tradition ; they were sometimes accustomed also to different legal systems ; and, in cases where they had previously been members of the majorities, they legitimately feared repression in return for the repression which their previous governments had exercised over the new majorities.

These treaties obtained, it must have seemed to the Jewish leaders at the conclusion of the Peace Conference that Jewry was entering on a new phase of peace and prosperity. The Jewish millions of Russia were enfranchised. Those who were to become subjects of the succession states of Russia and Austria were guaranteed freedom to develop their own culture, maintain their own schools, and at the same time enjoy full equality as citizens, and full access to all careers in the new states. For those who desired to re-establish themselves as a separate and recognized Jewish community, there existed the Balfour Declaration, with the prospect of a Palestinian home under British guarantee, recognized by the rest of the Allies, and ultimately by the League of Nations. The Jews of the west were united to their fellow-citizens by common sacrifices in the war, and by the Jewish and Christian names which stood side by side on the war memorials of every country.

It is true that there was a reverse to the picture. The Jews of the late Russian Empire were in a pitiable condition. Their homes had been devastated by the war ; their livelihoods had been destroyed ; thousands were homeless and penniless refugees, for whose relief enormous sums had been collected, especially in Britain and America. Even the conclusion of hostilities had brought them little respite ; the suspicion of the Poles had turned to violence throughout the country ; their entry into possession of lately Russian towns and villages had often been accompanied by the massacre of the Jewish populations and the complete destruction of the Jewish quarter. In Russia itself the little Jewish traders were the obvious antithesis of any communistic ideal and suffered accordingly as wicked capitalists ; while all through the provinces in which the White Russians were fighting with Allied help a losing battle against Bolshevism, Jews were massacred by tens of thousands as Bolsheviks. The future might indeed seem rosy, for these tragedies appeared but the final offshoots of the major tragedy of the war, but the actual circumstances of Jewry in 1919 were far from prosperous.

But fate had yet another poisoned dart in her quiver for this unhappy people. It has already been explained that it was inevitable that the Russian Revolution should bring them into prominence. The same thing happened, for much the same reasons, in other countries which passed through a period of proletarian revolution after the collapse of war. Where a high percentage of men in leading positions in these revolutions were Jewish, it was an easy and natural assumption that at least the same proportion were followers. Communism was widely proclaimed a *Jewish* plot. The fact that the mass of the Jews are intensely *bourgeois* was forgotten ; the percentage who were communist were taken as typical of the whole.

This prominence in the communist revolutions, coupled with the granting of the Balfour Declaration and the activities of Jews in the evolution of the Minority Treaties, led to the widespread acceptance of a curious document, *The Protocols of the Elders of Zion*, which, in saner times, would have been dismissed as a bad joke.

At the beginning of the twentieth century, when the Russian Government was looking for every argument with which to stave off reform, there was prepared in the office maintained by the Russian police in Paris, a forgery which purported to be a series of lectures to initiates describing the methods by which Jewry aimed at the complete overthrow of all Gentile governments and the substitution of a Jewish world empire. Its immediate purpose was to suggest that any demand for change or for reform was nothing but a Jewish manœuvre. The document was prepared in French and translated into Russian by a perfectly sincere but fanatical and rather unbalanced mystic of the name of Sergei Nilus. It went through several editions before the war, but had very little effect, even with the circles for whom it was intended. But after the Russian Revolution, it was widely circulated among the counter-revolutionaries, and the prominence of Trotsky and other Jewish Bolsheviks lent it an unexpected air of plausibility. The general horror with which the Bolshevik Revolution and the atrocities which accompanied it were regarded, and the presence of Jews in the other revolutions, both provided fertile soil for the acceptance of this document throughout Europe and America. It was first reprinted in Germany which was suffering under the humiliation of defeat and very ready to find the reason in an alien and sinister plot rather than in the failure of her own people, then in Poland, England, France, and almost simultaneously in America ; and everywhere it found a number of adherents.

Jews themselves first regarded it with such contempt that they did not even trouble to issue a denial of its authenticity. Fortunately at the time when it began to be a serious menace, the original from which it was forged was discovered accidentally by the correspondent of *The Times* at Constantinople, in a satire on the autocracy and ambitions of Napoleon III. The author, Maurice Joly, a French Catholic, had disguised his purpose in an imaginary dialogue between Montesquieu and Machiavelli, in which Machiavelli explains how easy it would be to overthrow the democracies of the nineteenth century and to establish an absolute autocracy in their place. Unhappily for the author he did not disguise his purpose sufficiently to deceive the police of Napoleon, and, although he published the book at Brussels, he paid for its appearance by eighteen months' imprisonment, and the suppression of his work. And the suppression was suffi-

ciently successful for the book to have almost
completely disappeared, so that the forgers
ran very little risk of their handiwork being
recognised, when they simply took Machiavelli's plans and ascribed them to " Elders
of Zion."

So far as most people were concerned the
discovery of this original—and more than
two-fifths of the document are taken textu-
ally from it—disposed of any alarm that they
may have felt at the disclosure of the existence
of a sinister Jewish plot against society.
Unhappily, the rapid growth of antisemitism after the war, for reasons which will be
discussed later, led to its continual reap-
pearance. It was too convenient to be discarded, and the fact of its complete exposure
was either tacitly ignored, or else dismissed
as unimportant. Yet even the most pessi-
mistic Jew could hardly have foreseen that
within fifteen years it would become officially
adopted and protected by the government
of a once great European country. At the
time of its emergence it would have seemed
absurd to allow it to obscure the era of prosperity and tranquillity upon which Jewry
appeared to be entering.

# CHAPTER VII

## DISILLUSION IN THE DISPERSION

THE years which have followed the Peace Conference have been years of tragic disillusion for the Jews of almost every country. None of the high hopes of 1919 have been fulfilled, and tragedies, which in 1919 would have been deemed absolutely outside the bounds of possibility, have fallen and are still falling on their unhappy heads. Whatever the failings of individual Jews, it is difficult to see how anyone can sincerely see in a people so sorely harassed, and so impotent to avert whatever fate may have in store for them, the secret would-be rulers of the world, the universal menace to Gentile society.

The first signs of what was to come appeared already with the demobilizations of the immense war-time armies. In the days when Berlin, Vienna and Budapest had been capitals of vast empires the prominence of Jews in certain walks of life had passed almost unnoticed. If many of the doctors, lawyers, journalists and business-men were Jews, there were almost unbounded openings for the sons of the middle and upper classes in the vast civil and military administrations which were much more attractive than business or the professions. But after the war young and middle-aged men, finding those openings much reduced in number, turned to just these occupations to make a living, and discovered the Jews to be uncomfortable rivals. To the demobilized soldiers was quickly added the wealthy class of *rentiers* who had previously lived prosperously on the income of industrial and public securities ; for the collapse of the currencies of Germany, Austria and Hungary reduced the value of these securities to nothing in a matter of months. It is difficult to-day to remember the time when the German mark fell to one million-millionth of its pre-war value. If the Austrian collapse to one fourteen-thousandth was less spectacular, it was equally decisive for the Austrians. There were few fortunes which when so reduced would yield enough for the poorest living to its possessor. One story will illustrate those days. There were two brothers in Vienna, both wealthy. One managed his fortune well, and when the collapse came he was reduced to beggary ; the other spent it all on wine and luxuries, and continued to live in modest comfort on the sale of empty bottles. In so topsy-turvy a world passions are easily roused, bitterness is quickly concentrated on any object supposed, on whatever evidence, to be responsible. The presence of Jews among those who successfully speculated in falling currencies, the fact that there were Jews who built up fortunes during these years of despair, immensely stimulated existing antisemitic feeling.

Similar conditions rapidly spread it into the coming generation, and that not in the defeated countries alone. Young Jews, with their traditional thirst for education, with the opportunities for it which they possessed as town-dwellers (a situation which gave them considerable advantage over the sons of peasants less accustomed to book-learning, and unable to pursue their studies without leaving home), and with the special enthusiasm of their new liberation, flocked to all the universities of Eastern Europe at last opened to them. In the first years of the Polish Republic they formed nearly 30 per cent. of the students.

Inevitably a problem was created. Youth is proverbially hot-headed. The young Poles also desired to enter the universities, and were filled with an enthusiastic desire for everything to be 100 per cent. Polish. In the past not merely their culture, but even their language had been suppressed. Russia had been everywhere, now nothing except Poland was to be anywhere. There was no place in their scheme of things for minorities—especially for Jews, since the other minorities were largely illiterate and poverty-stricken peasants and consequently not prominent at the universities or in the professional and intellectual life of the nation. In a very short time an economic argument was added to this ideological enthusiasm. The fact that education was free had brought far more young men and women to the universities than the country could afford to maintain in its professions and public services. Graduation was easy, the discovery of a job for the graduate was extremely difficult. It is not surprising that ex-students were easily won by propaganda which preached to them that there would be jobs for all if they were not monopolized by the Jews—incidentally it was from this unemployed graduate class in Germany that Hitler obtained many of his first supporters.

What was true of Poland was true of almost every other new country. Nowhere perhaps was the economic crisis more acutely felt than in Hungary. She had lost the whole of her empire—two-thirds of her territory. Magyars seeking work poured into Budapest from all the lost provinces—and in Hungary there had also been the interlude of the communistic republic of Bela Kun, in which a high percentage of the leaders were Jews. The demand was made that Jewish access to the universities, and so to the professions, should be strictly limited by a *numerus clausus* (paragraph regulating numbers) in accordance with the proportion of Jews in the general population. A bill was actually introduced for this purpose. Largely through the energetic action of British Jews this law was declared contrary to the Minority Treaty which Hungary had signed. But though it was formally repealed, it pointed the way to a solution which was quickly imitated by private and unofficial action. Limitation of access to the universities or to particular faculties was frequently necessary, and it could easily be operated in such a way that the students refused admission should be precisely the Jewish candidates.

While the existence of the Minority Treaties prevented such action from being officially recognized, it was the conditions guaranteed by these treaties which gave it a certain moral respectability. It was natural and proper that these countries should make strenuous efforts either to rebuild their own cultures, which had for long periods been eclipsed by foreign domination, or to create homogeneous units out of the relics of polyglot empires, and it was too much to expect them to allow unlimited access to positions of importance in the political and cultural life of the nation to groups which insisted on their legal right to maintain their own language, their own culture, and their own separate identity.

The question of access to the universities was a real conflict of two rights, or rather it would have been, but for two developments. In the first place the actual Jewish student was not to blame for the situation, and the violence which manifested itself in the immediate post-war years, leading to frequent assaults and occasional fatalities, was a blot on the academic honour of nearly every one of the new states. In the second place, it was futile to resent the rush of Jewish students to the universities, when no other openings were offered them. Legal equality turned out to be a poor substitute for actual liberty to enter every walk of national life, and there was truth in the statement of a President of the Jewish Students' Union of Warsaw

University who remarked bitterly : " if they would allow us to be porters and tram-conductors, half of us would never have tried to be students."

So narrow, however, were the actual openings for Jewish youth that the partial closing of Eastern European universities only provided a temporary alleviation of the economic struggle. Thousands of young Jews went abroad from Poland, Rumania and elsewhere to study in Germany, Italy, France and other countries ; and they came back to their native lands, often with better qualifications than they could have obtained at home, to seek entrance into the professions for which they had prepared themselves. Difficulties were put in the way of accepting foreign diplomas, but the flood continued. Tragic though it is, it is not surprising that the universities of the post-war world have been the centres, not of free competition and academic calm, but of the bitterest antisemitism ; that students have provided the leaders of almost every antisemitic movement ; and that they have been the actual perpetrators of many of the political assassinations with which anti-semitism has marked the stages of its progress. Walter Rathenau, the brilliant Jewish economist and politician who did much for

Germany's economy during and after the war, was assassinated by members of a group consisting largely of students in 1922. In both Poland and Rumania students have been brazenly acquitted for the murder of Jews, or of prominent politicians suspected of pro-Jewish sympathies, and have become national heroes for their acts.

The bitter economic conflict, together with violent persecution by the nationalist groups, had the inevitable consequence of driving more and more young Jews into the parties of the left. The attitudes of Socialist and Jewish student organizations towards the groups of the right were often identical, and left-wing groups prided themselves on their freedom from antisemitic prejudice. But the consequence was naturally an intensification of the antisemitism of the nationalists who could proclaim that their suspicion of the political reliability of the Jew was triumphantly vindicated.

And all the time the exclusion of the Jew from almost every public post was maintained, and tended to be intensified rather than relaxed. In an old-established country, where far more is left to private enterprise than to government monopoly, this exclusion does not sound very serious, but in new countries the modernization and development of economic life is largely in the hands of the government which alone controls the requisite capital. In such conditions government monopolies abound ; whole industries are under government control ; railways and transport, with their enormous demand for capital, are government affairs. Exclusion from public posts in these countries is a tremendous limitation of opportunities.

How serious such a situation was for Jewry as a whole can be seen from the demographic and economical distribution of Jews in the post-war world. In Germany and countries to the west and south of Germany, and in the United States the Jewish population had remained stationary since the outbreak of war in 1914 had closed the doors of emigration from Russia. East of Germany the Jewish population had undergone immense transformations in political allegiance, and there had been a good deal of actual movement, but few " Eastern European " Jews had been able to escape altogether from that part of the world. The flight from the battle-areas of the eastern front had added considerably to the Jewries of Vienna and Budapest, with the result that the tiny post-war states of Austria and Hungary found themselves with 230,000 and 477,000 Jews, respectively, forming 3·5 and 5·6 per cent. of their populations. A smaller stream had fled south-eastwards into Rumania and westwards into what was to become Poland. As Rumania also acquired territories from Russia, Austria and Hungary in all of which Jews were numerous, the Jewish population of that country rose from 250,000 in 1910 to 900,000 in 1927. But both in numbers and in proportion to the total population, the country which inherited the most Jews was Poland. Of the twenty-seven millions within her frontiers little more than eighteen were actual Poles ; of her minorities the Jews formed not less than three million.

Over four and a half million Jews were, therefore, affected by the attitude of these four countries. In all of them both the governments and the student population viewed them with hostility. In Poland, though the Jewish population was 10 per cent. of the whole, Jews formed only 1 per cent. of the innumerable officials of the government. In Rumania more than half the Jewish population did not even succeed in obtaining citizenship, let alone government employment.

The unhappy position of these Jews was

still further emphasized by the anomalies of their economic distribution, which made them appear to be much more influential in the life of the nation than they really were. Had the Jewish population been anything like equally distributed throughout the country and its different occupations, even the 10 per cent. of Poland would have scarcely been noticed, and in one way or another most or all of them would have found a living. But both history and politics prevented this from happening. Middle-class Jews, excluded from government service, had only the " free professions " of medicine, law and journalism open to them. They flocked to these professions, as they had to the university faculties which prepared for them. Their proportion among doctors, lawyers and journalists was inevitably conspicuous, and the professional classes followed the students in becoming an easy prey to antisemitic agitation. Middle-class unions repeatedly petitioned their governments to exclude Jews from their professions, and, where they were free to do so, sometimes actually expelled their Jewish members themselves.

In actual fact these professions were almost everywhere too crowded for the moral health of the communities concerned. Where there are too many lawyers or doctors for all to obtain a decent standard of living, there will always be an overwhelming temptation for many to lower their standards of professional conduct in order to attract clients. In any country where antisemitism is current, there will be an equally irresistible temptation to associate unprofessional conduct exclusively with the Jewish members of the professions, and there will always be sufficient actual and concrete examples to support the association. It is noteworthy that even in the United States the continual flood of Jewish graduates into the professions of medicine and law meets a great deal of resentment. American Jewish medical students are to be found in almost every medical faculty throughout the world, because of the difficulties put in their way when they seek access to the medical faculties of American universities ; and yet there is no American medical faculty without a fair proportion of Jews.

The importance of this last fact is that it shows that it is not wholly exclusion from other professions which moves the young Jew of Eastern Europe to seek a career in medicine. The same fact exists in the United States where all professions are open to Jews.

Medicine and law are age-long traditions in Jewry, and it is one of the services of Zionism to the Jewries of the Dispersion that it continually encourages young Jews to seek to broaden the occupational basis of the Jewish community. Yet it is certainly true that politics and jealousy make this broadening process infinitely slow, and tend to tie the coming generation to the paths successfully trodden in a more easy-going period by their fathers.

If politics, jealousy and tradition made life difficult for the Jew who entered the professions, exactly the same disadvantages beset his commercial neighbour. Concentration was a feature of Jewish commercial life long before Jews were admitted to the professions at all, but the reasons for it were the same : their exclusion from other walks of life. History has compelled them to keep their economic eggs in the minimum number of baskets, and when the compulsion of legal exclusion was lifted, social and religious arguments took their place. Jewish life is naturally communal life ; the permanent pressure of a hostile majority outside tends to make Jews keep together and help one another. Mixed employment with Gentiles made the observance of different religious

153

holidays, and especially of a different weekly day of rest, difficult for observing Jews. Even Jewish employers often had to choose between an entirely Jewish and an entirely Gentile personnel—and chose the latter.

The result of this concentration is inevitably the rise of Jewish monopolies or quasi-monopolies. If Jews take up the tobacco trade it will soon be proclaimed that all or almost all the trade is in their hands. This was the case in Poland at the beginning of her independent existence. A very high proportion of the manufacturers of cigars and cigarettes, and quite a high proportion of the workers, were Jewish. The tobacco industry became a government monopoly, and the number of Jewish merchants and workers affected was out of all proportion to their general proportion in the country At the same time, seeking for a means of giving a livelihood to men disabled in her wars, Poland decided to give them a monopoly of retailing tobacco. Again far more than 10 per cent. of those who lost their licences to these new vendors were Jews. In the clothing industry, in all its varied branches, Jews have taken an extraordinarily prominent part in almost every country. In Poland over 40 per cent. of those engaged in this industry are Jews, and it was their great-uncles and cousins who established much of the cheap clothing industry in England, almost all of it in the United States, and a considerable proportion in Germany and elsewhere. In Poland again over 60 per cent. of the shopkeepers were Jewish until the growth of Polish co-operatives, which refused to employ Jews, diminished it. Of the commercial travellers, commercial agents, and other undefined persons hanging on the skirts of commerce, 80 per cent. were Jewish at the end of the war. Such a class thrives on the laziness and ignorance of the landowners and peasants. Every advance in education and thrift, in co-operatives and technical education, lessens its opportunities of gaining a living. Brought into being more by the faults of others than by any traditional ingenuity, its interests and those of the country are apt to be diametrically opposed to each other. Looked on as an anti-social element in the population, it receives neither pity nor assistance in finding other occupations as progress robs it of its accustomed livelihood. Jews of this class were the universal moneylenders of the local landowners, and often of the peasant. They bought and sold everything for aristocrats too lazy and too proud to manage their own affairs ; and this situation was almost as common in Rumania and Hungary as it was in Poland.

The poverty and improvidence of their debtors, together with the insecurity created by popular and governmental hostility augmented their rates of interest to usurious levels, and this in turn provided ready propaganda for antisemitic agitation. That the fault lay primarily with the debtor and not with specific Jewish qualities is revealed by the fact that the peasantry of such countries as Ireland and India are equally thoroughly exploited by usurers and " agents," although there are practically no Jews in those countries ; and the proud and extravagant aristocrats of eighteenth-century England were as indebted to their tradesmen and attorneys as those of Poland to their Jewish factors.

The general result of all these conditions in Eastern Europe is that the Jewish communities become more and more impoverished. Their opportunities dwindle, and it is often for the general advantage that they should. But nothing whatever is done to assist them to find new and useful functions in society. Practically all doors are closed to would-be emigrants ; only tiny trickles to Palestine or

America replace the immense floods of pre-war days.

In such circumstances work of the utmost value is done by international and national Jewish organizations which labour for the re-orientation of the Jewish population, introducing technical and agricultural schools, credit banks, loan funds, and every kind of organization for enabling Jews to enter into the productive life of their countries. But such efforts are voluntary in their finances, and even the most generous charity can only touch a fringe of the problem. For the bulk of Eastern European Jewry no salvation is yet in sight.

The situation is made worse by the fact that an economic decline due to natural causes has been accompanied by a steady increase of antisemitism in every section of the non-Jewish community. In Poland particularly physical violence against the Jews has become almost a daily occurrence. Political agitators have spread from the towns to the villages, and general poverty and widespread unemployment have provided fertile breeding grounds for antisemitic agitation. During the same period nationalist parties on the German model, often with German support and encouragement, have clamoured for a

" radical " solution on German lines. As usual the students have been the pioneers of extremism, but similar views to-day are penetrating more and more into every class of society. And what has for some time been threatening in Poland has already taken place in Hungary. A law, far more rigorous than that forbidden in the days when Minority Treaties were still respected, was passed in the spring of 1939 by which the participation of the Jews in the public, cultural and economic life of the country was limited to a fixed percentage. One incident connected with its passage shows the fantastic times in which we live. The Prime Minister, Bela Imredy, who proposed it, defended it as the inevitable response to the call of the old Hungarian blood in his veins. Before it passed he was obliged to resign because he discovered that he had overlooked the old Jewish blood in his veins, acquired from his great-grandfather.

While, thus, a general picture of Eastern European Jewry must inevitably be painted in sombre colours, it must not be thought that this section of Jewry has been nothing but an unwanted liability to the countries where it dwells. It is true that historical circumstances have not been favourable to the development of a sturdy and independent Jewish stock, and that modern developments have wrought havoc with the place which these Jews occupied; yet they fulfilled an essential role in what are still primitive and undeveloped societies. Without their loans many peasants would have been unable to carry on between seed-time and harvest; without their "flair" markets would have remained undeveloped, goods wasted for lack of knowledge where or how to sell them, and estates left to the complete mismanagement of ignorant and lazy landowners.

Nor is this all. Eastern Europe owes to Jews a very large share of the introduction of health and social services. The very fact that insuperable difficulties were often placed in the way of medical students in native universities, enabled young Jews to get much superior training in the better equipped and more advanced colleges of Germany, Austria or Switzerland, and to return to endow their own countries with the latest discoveries of western science. Similarly in banking and journalism, in business and manufacturing, Jews contributed to the general raising of the standard of living by their introduction of modern technique and knowledge, and by their contacts with the western world. They found markets abroad and introduced new goods at home ; they organized banking and they facilitated credit. While the introduction of the cinema and American film may be considered a mixed blessing, they have also been prominent as patrons of art and music, and without their interest it would be difficult for many cultural activities in Eastern Europe to make their way.

In some of these fields they are still indispensable, and it is noteworthy that when Octavian Goga tried to set up a government in Rumania on the model of that of Germany, it lasted only forty-five days. That period was sufficient to convince the country that she could not treat her Jews in the German manner without totally dislocating her own economic machinery.

What is true of the great Jewries of Central and Eastern Europe is true also of the Jewish populations in other countries in that area. There are the same concentrations, the same difficulties, and the same uncertain future. In Lithuania there are 160,000 Jews out of a population of just over two millions, in Latvia, 100,000 out of just under that figure. In both countries there is less deliberate hostility than in Poland and Rumania, but in both also the antisemitic movement has tended to grow rather than diminish, and the maladjustment of the Jews to become more and more noticeable as standards improve and, at the same, the world situation leads to high unemployment figures for all classes of workers. Out of the 14,000,000 inhabitants of Czechoslovakia before her disappearance there were 354,000 Jews, the most prosperous community of any in Central Europe, and the least subject to antisemitism, except among the German and Hungarian minorities. What will be the future for them in the new German Protectorate it is only too easy to prophesy, for the fate of their brothers in Germany will inevitably be theirs.

Compared with these countries where the outlook is dark, the number of European Jews living in countries still unaffected by antisemitism is few, and has been still further diminished by the new racial policy of Italy. The Rome-Berlin axis has forced Mussolini, who only a few years ago poured contempt on the idea that Italy could possibly become antisemitic, to come into line with German ideas on the subject. Less than a hundred thousand Jews, half-Jews and persons of Jewish origin are affected, but it is not merely a question of numbers. That the Jews should suddenly be discovered to be an alien and intolerable element in Fascist Italy after not merely two thousand years of residence in the country, but after more than fifteen years of full co-operation in the Fascist party, has struck a blow at the security of Jews everywhere else in Europe. If such a *volte face* is possible there, they may well ask : what is our security in Holland, in Scandinavia, in France or in Great Britain ?

Quite apart from the rest of European Jewries stand the three million Jews of Soviet Russia. The immense majority of them belonged in 1917 to the class which Communism was most anxious to suppress, the class of petty traders, minor " capitalists " and bourgeois professionals. Their adjustment to the new conceptions of life and society was, therefore, both slow and difficult. The first years of the revolution left them ruined and utterly bewildered. Apart from the few whom politics or education had brought within the immense machinery of government, they could find few means of adapting their occupations to communistic demands. The introduction of the " New Economic Policy " in 1921 with its allowance of private trading seemed to offer them a respite, but its duration was short-lived. Only one group of the Jewish population found it relatively easy to adapt itself to new surroundings ; these were the Jewish farmers and peasants, colonies of whom were to be found in the Crimea, the Ukraine, and other portions of the south-west. Where the colonies formed compact and homogeneous groups they were allowed to form their own " Soviets," with Yiddish as the official language, and with Jews occupying all official positions. In some cases Yiddish became the official language of whole districts where the proportion of Jewish village Soviets was high enough. Schools and libraries, concerts and theatres were Jewish in their content and outlook, and no attempt was made to suppress Jewish culture—within the general Soviet scheme of things, by which Judaism itself was as much forbidden as any other religion.

Not only were the colonies readily admitted to self-government, but movement from the crowded quarters of the Pale to these Jewish communes was encouraged ; and in 1928 a still more ambitious attempt was made to create Jewish communal life and autonomy. A large and little populated province in the extreme east of the Soviet

Union, bordering Manchukuo, was given to the Jews for settlement as an autonomous Jewish republic. Here in Biro-Bidzhan they were to forget the miseries of the Pale—and the glories of Zion. For the Soviets consider Zionism to be but a weapon of British Imperialism, and all contact with the Zionist Organization or the settlement of Palestine is absolutely forbidden.

It is too early to say whether the experiment in Biro-Bidzhan will be a success. The province is very remote, its geographical situation makes it likely to be the battlefield of any Russo-Japanese conflict, and most of its riches are still to be conquered. Pioneering of this kind is absolutely unfamiliar to Russian Jews, and they must be given time to adapt themselves to it. A start has certainly been made, but so far only a few tens of thousands have been able to find a permanent settlement there, in spite of the lavish sums placed at the disposal of the authorities of the province by the Soviet Union, and the efforts to forward agricultural training undertaken by international Jewish organizations, especially the Joint Distribution Committee of the United States. Unhappily the Russian Government absolutely refuses to open its doors to refugees from other countries, so that this territory at present offers no possible asylum to the fugitives from Nazi philosophy or Polish economics.

To complete this survey of modern Jewry, a word needs to be said of the situation outside Europe. The European continent, together with the U.S.S.R., includes about nine million Jews, that is 60 per cent. of the Jews of the world. The next largest group, the American, contains about half this number. Jews are to be found scattered throughout the length and breadth of the two parts of the continent, but the community of the United States easily outnumbers those of all the other countries together, for it contains over four million out of a total of under five. Most of the Jewries have the same mixed origin. The oldest groups, now extremely small, were Spanish, spreading from the Spanish and Portuguese colonies of Latin America, and they still attract a certain number of Levantine and similar Jews, because of the community of language. In the middle of the nineteenth century there was a new wave from Germany, but as this only brought the figures of the Jewry of the United States up to about 50,000 by 1848, and 230,000 by 1880, the origin of the main

American Jewish population can be seen to be the Russian pogroms. Since 1933 there has been a second exodus of German Jews to America, but the general restriction of immigration since the war has confined this flow to relatively small figures.

The particular interest of American Jewry is that is has been able to develop in relatively virgin soil, and with extremely little restriction on its activities. It is therefore possible to see what happens to a community which has lived an artificial life for centuries when the restrictions are removed. The most striking feature of the picture is that in every American country there are Jews engaged in agriculture, although the general trend of the age is away from the land. In Argentine and Brazil these agricultural colonies are the direct result of the deliberate action of the Jewish Colonization Association, which owns considerable tracts of land in both countries. But this does not explain the 10,000 Jewish farmers of the United States or the 700 of Canada. These figures represent, of course, but small percentages of the Jewish populations, but they are nevertheless significant. They are also significant as evidence of the innate conservatism of human nature, since they show that the immense majority of young Jews seek the environment familiar to the older generations. They came from urban centres ; in urban centres most of them live. They were accustomed to crowded quarters, and nearly three-quarters of all the Jews of the United States live in eleven towns. Outside the States, by far the larger proportion of the other Jewries are also concentrated in the capital or chief commercial cities of the continent.

This concentration is equally observable in their occupations. It has already been said that so many turn to medicine that American Universities officially or unofficially restrict their numbers and compel young Jews to seek their medical training elsewhere. They are equally numerous in the law. Their speculative initiative has been shown more by such occupations as real-estate dealing, and the development of new kinds of stores, than by any preponderance in pure finance. The part that they play in the banking and stock exchange life of New York is nothing abnormal, when it is realized that they form nearly a third of the population of that city. On the other hand here, as in Poland and Russia whence the parents of so many came, their distribution in business is extraordinarily uneven. Catering and clothing are very largely Jewish occupations, while in steel and iron, two huge national industries, hardly any Jews are either employees or employers.

In the rest of the continent the same facts would emerge, though in this case the highest Jewish percentages would be found in shop- and store-keeping, since industries are much less developed. In other words, the new world got her farmers and pioneers from the countrysides of Europe, her town-dwellers from the towns, and it is only slowly that the character of a family changes as a result of a new environment. That many families have come from the country to the towns does not contradict this, since exactly the same thing has been happening in Europe.

On the whole it can be claimed that the Jewries of America, especially those of the United States, have prospered. History has enabled the Jew to adapt himself to new environments—even if it takes the form of finding the same niche in the new society that he had had in the old—and this has stood him in good stead in a situation where a whole continent was improvising a new existence. For if the Jewish population of the United States grew from 50,000 to over four million between 1850 and 1920, it must be remembered that the total population grew from twenty-three millions to one hundred and five millions during the same time. The wealth of American Jewry has been the saviour of their European brethren during the last twenty-five years. Millions of dollars have been collected annually for the relief of distress, first in Russia, Poland and Rumania, then, since 1933, in Germany; and in addition American Jews have provided enormous sums for the building up of the National Home in Palestine. Though criticism is levelled—often unjustly—at the way in which the Jew acquires wealth, there can be nothing but praise for the generosity with which he contributes it to worthy causes, for besides these sums contributed for specifically Jewish purposes, the same Jewries have certainly given their full share to public causes with no special Jewish interest.

Compared with the Jewries of America, those of Africa and Asia are very small. The wealthiest group is that of the Union of South Africa, for many Jews took part in the scramble for gold and diamonds during the latter part of the nineteenth century, and—as with Gentiles—some acquired immense fortunes, and some graves. Of the former group some—also as with Gentiles—were not very scrupulous as to how they acquired it, and very ostentatious of it when acquired. The result has been that the South African Jewry has attracted to itself a good deal of antisemitic feeling, and since Jews form over 4 per cent. of the white population in a relatively small community they are inevitably somewhat conspicuous.

The most prosperous of the North African Jews are in Egypt, where the community numbers some 72,000 out of a total population of sixteen millions. Higher in proportion to the general populations, but infinitely lower in wealth, are the great Jewries of the French possessions of North Africa—161,000 in Morocco, 110,000 in Algiers, and 60,000 in Tunis. These Jews are partly indigenous, and partly descendants of the refugees from the expulsion from Spain and Portugal at the end of the fifteenth century. Under Mohammedan rulers they were bitterly oppressed and they were treated with disgust and contempt by the native Moslems. They were herded together in ghettoes, made to wear special dress, and excluded from most honourable callings. The result is that they are still a thoroughly impoverished and down-trodden group. Although there are a certain number of rich merchants among them, the bulk are unskilled and poverty-stricken artisans and labourers.

An African group of Jews of particular interest at the present time is the Falasha community of Abyssinia. These Jews are not Semites but negroes, and their conversion to Judaism is, in legend, supposed to date from the return of the Queen of Sheba (from whom the Emperor Haile Selassie traces his descent) from her visit to Solomon. Certainly it dates back to the pre-Christian era. The Falashas maintained an autonomous Jewish kingdom until the seventeenth century, when they were defeated by the Christian Abyssinians, and they still number 50,000. It would appear from recent pronouncements that they are now going to be treated as the lowest class of the Abyssinian population, a piece of meaningless vindictiveness, since they possess none of the qualities by which " the Jews " are said to exploit races among whom they live. The Falashas are farmers and artisans, and refuse to indulge in commerce, which they consider to be contrary to the Law of Moses.

In Asia, apart from Palestine, there are only two Jewries of any considerable historic importance, in Baghdad and in Perisa. While many of the Jews in these two centres could best be compared to the Jews of Morocco and Algiers, they contain a larger proportion of great merchants, and many of the rich Jewish families of India, Singapore, Hong-Kong and elsewhere came originally from either Persia or Baghdad.

In all, the Jews of these two continents form less than 10 per cent. of the world's Jewish population, and their importance in Jewish life is even less. Nevertheless in the last five years there has been a steady trickle of German Jews to all these parts, and they have offered at least the haven of obscurity, and the hope of the avoidance of anti-semitism of the Central or Eastern European variety.

It is on the European situation that the barometer of Jewish life is set. It is to Europe that the stream of American Jewish charity is mainly directed ; it is only *refugees* from Europe who turn naturally to Africa or Asia. Prosperity in America, obscurity in Asia cannot modify the general verdict on the history of the past twenty years, that it has been a period of increasing gloom in Jewry. History and contemporary events have conspired together. A population ill-adjusted to the changes of modern life in its economic structure, has been denied the necessary assistance for its re-adjustment by the growth of nationalism, while the disease of anti-semitism has struck at both poor and prosperous alike.

# CHAPTER VIII

### THE CATASTROPHE IN GERMANY

It would be difficult to find in history a
parallel to the persecution from which Jews
and those with Jewish blood have suffered
since the advent of the National-Socialist
Party to power in Germany in the beginning
of 1933. There are pages smeared with
more blood, but none with so many tears.
The Jews themselves have suffered bloodier
catastrophes, even in the twentieth century,
but no people has ever been submitted to a
more ruthless, brutal and all-pervading agony.
It has long since ceased to be " news " except
when some sudden act of brutality, such as
the pogrom and fine inflicted in November
1938 for the shooting of Vom Rath, the
German official in Paris, provides good head-
lines ; but the events which shocked the
world in 1933 were but a prelude to the
quieter, but far more sinister administrative
and party actions which have followed without a break for a period of more than six

years, and show no signs of any relaxation so long as the regime endures.

Bitter persecution and outbreaks of ferocious cruelty are often associated in history with the violent feelings aroused in war, or with the Sadism of an individual. The tens of thousands of Jews who perished in the Ukraine in 1919 and 1920 died in the midst of the horrors of civil war ; the cruelties of Nero ceased with his death and were regarded with detestation by his own Romans during his lifetime. The deepest tragedy of the present persecution in Germany is that it is carried through by the deliberate actions of tens of thousands of normal individuals, school-masters, judges, doctors, professors, business-men, local authorities, without question and without protest, on the instructions of the Government or the Party ; and, in so far as they are aware of what is happening, it is accepted as right and proper, as natural and inevitable by the great bulk of the population.

Conventional explanations, referring to " gangster rule," " Sadistic leaders," " economic jealousy," are not enough to account for so extraordinary a situation, and it would indeed be impossible within the limits of this book to give a reasoned explanation of the whole background and meaning of the phenomenon. Yet something must be attempted, for otherwise the story is not only inexplicable but also incredible.

In the first place it was possible for National-Socialist philosophy with its adoration of unity and discipline to obtain such a hold in Germany just because Germany itself, as a geographical entity, lacks definition or coherence. Since no sea with its precise boundaries surrounds Germany, there has been a natural longing among the Germans to seek by deliberate action that which nature has denied. Coherence has not grown automatically as it has in English history. The admiration of force has the same origin. For centuries Germany, divided into an ever shifting multitude of petty states, could play no part worthy of her culture or her manpower in European life. She always felt humiliated by her lack of force—and consequently she worships force.

To these general considerations must be added conditions special to the situation in 1933. The long economic depression which began in 1929 struck Germany with especial violence because she had not yet really recovered her balance from the psychological and economic effects of defeat. Six million unemployed—for that was the figure when Hitler came to power—was more than she could bear. In the German mind it showed that the *whole* course which had been followed since 1919 was wrong, for she was in no mood for nice distinctions.

While these were factors which made the people turn a kindlier eye on the struttings and bullyings of National-Socialist agitators than would otherwise have been the case amongst a people essentially cultured and friendly, another factor disposed them to accept the antisemitism which was a fundamental part of National-Socialist philosophy from the very beginning. Defeat in 1918 was all the bitterer in that for a brief period she had tasted the power and the unity for which she had long dreamed. She fell from a pedestal which she had only just mounted. In such a neurosis it was balm—perhaps the only possible balm—to be told that her fall was due to no mistakes of her own, but to a stab in the back from an *alien* enemy ; that it was no dishonour to her own people ; it was the act of strangers—of Jews. To the same group could, with equal ease, be ascribed the long and weary years of failure through which—looking back—she was convinced that she had passed since the war.

All her troubles—all of them, she felt—were due to the Jews. So it was easy to convince her that only by the complete elimination of the poison of Jewry could the unity and the power which she had lost be recovered.

On such a basis it is easier to understand the first outbreaks against the Jews which accompanied Hitler's assumption of power, but what of its ruthless continuation long after any possible influence of the Jews was eliminated ? The answer is to be found both in the continual propaganda with which a dictatorship is obliged to keep its people quiet, and in the German tendency to standardize everything into a philosophic system. The individual cruelties, the sufferings of individual Jews, however regrettable, are looked on as the inevitable consequences of the National Socialist outlook on life (the untranslatable German word: *Weltanschauung*). A young German sailor who was ranting against the Jews was once asked what he had himself suffered from them. He replied that he had only met one in his life, who lived in his native village and was universally respected. When asked why, then, he so abused them, he replied with the conviction that the answer was totally adequate : " but that is part of our *Weltanschauung*."

Another story will illustrate a final point. A cultured and substantial business man, not a member of the Party, excused all the persecution of the Jews with the phrase, " but it is a war between us and the Jews, and in war there are casualties ; it is a pity, but it cannot be otherwise." To the out-sider the idea that it is necessary for 80,000,000 to wage a war of such dimensions against a minority of less than 1 per cent—for there were less than 600,000 Jews in Germany in 1933, and including " non-Aryans " the number is apparently at most about a million and a half—is fantastic and revolting. Even to-day, with the addition of Austrian and Czechoslovak Jewries the proportion is little if any higher, for the Jewry of old Germany has dwindled to about a quarter of a million. But National-Socialism has personified in " the Jew " everything which was decadent or anti-social in modern civilization. And there were always sufficient individual Jews in the activity concerned to give a show of reason to the attack. Communism was a dangerous enemy, and there were Jews among the Communists ; the immorality of Berlin was notorious, and there were Jews who kept brothels and published pornographic literature ; pacifism was unmanly, and there were Jewish pacifists ; speculation was unpatriotic, and there were prominent Jewish speculators. These ideas were transferred to every other walk of life. Law, history, medicine, art, even pure science were proclaimed to have had seeds of Jewish corruption in them under the post-war republic, and to need purification — *Aryanization* — before they could be fitted for national use.

Yet, when all is said in explanation, the fact remains that an explanation is not an excuse. Only in an entirely deterministic world is it true that " *tout savoir, c'est tout pardonner* ". Germany has nothing to fear from the vengeance of the Jews ; they are not, and never have been in any position to inflict more than pin-pricks. But, though she despises the verdict of contemporary humanity, she cannot evade the judgment of history. All has been done deliberately and in cold blood. Facts have been distorted in every realm of knowledge to support a theory which its own originators know to be untrue. Every noble human emotion has been prostituted, until it is impossible to say which is the more terrible, the unrelenting persecution of unoffending Jews, or the deliberate poisoning of the minds of innocent Germans.

Hitler obtained complete power on March 23, 1933. Already on April 7 all Jews and persons who had one Jewish grandparent were expelled from all government employment; and this included not only central but local officials down to the humblest, and in government employment of every kind. By an addition of the 6th of May all university professors and teachers, all school teachers, and all judges were treated in the same way. On the 22nd of April all panel doctors of "non-Aryan" origin were likewise expelled, and as the greater part of a German doctor's patients belong to "panels," this was a severe blow to their livelihood. At first those who had held position before the war, or who had fought in the war, or whose sons or fathers had been killed in the war, were allowed to remain—by the government, but in such cases it was left to the Party to make their positions impossible. This interaction of Party and Government is part of a deliberate plan, culminating in Hitler's own words at Nuremberg in 1935 that if the law which disenfranchised the Jews completely did not suffice to humble them, the Jewish question would be handed over to the Party for definite solution.

Party and Government played this game

together in the very first days, as they play it still. Immediately after the assumption of power the Party demanded the complete boycott of the Jews. In response to the unalterable will of the Party, the Government decreed the boycott of April 1. When the Party does not act, the Press can always do so for it. Again and again the Press, controlled directly by the Government and Party, has demanded violent measures of one kind or another, and the Government then takes the action demanded, so as to protect the victims from the natural indignation of the Party.

In May and June similar attacks were made on Jews in all branches of the legal profession ; in June dentists were treated in the same way as doctors ; in the summer and autumn of 1933 and in the spring of 1934 a clean sweep was made of Jewish journalists and editors, musicians, actors, artists, and broadcasters ; during the same time Jews were expelled from the cinema industry, and Germany not only refused to allow any Jew to act in German films, but refuses to admit from any country films in which Jews play prominent parts.

All this was done before any general regulation of Jewish status was issued ; the

Jews affected by this legislation were still nominally citizens, except where they had been explicitly deprived of their civic rights and made " outlaws." This has happened in a few cases also to distinguished German " Aryans " such as Thomas Mann, but it has not only happened to Jews such as Einstein and Ernst Toller, but also in a host of other cases to Jews who were not prominent in any walk of life. Outlawry enables the State to confiscate the property of the outlaw. But at the end of more than two years of this spasmodic and irregular attack, a definite decision was made at the Party Rally at Nuremberg in September 1935. By the " Nuremberg Laws " the Jews were reduced from the status of citizens to that of subjects. And to this indignity was added the insult that no German woman of child-bearing age might serve as domestic to a Jew, " in case he might pollute her blood." This " precaution " was subsequently extended to secretaries and certain categories of office workers.

In March 1936 pharmacists and druggists were attacked, and in July Jewish rag-dealers were added to the growing class of those whose " political unreliability " made it dangerous for them to ply their trade un-

interrupted in Germany. In September
architects—because they were accused of
introducing " oriental " flat-topped houses
into the German landscape—in October
art dealers, in January 1937 booksellers,
in February 1938 auctioneers, and in June
brokers and estate managers came under the
axe. Finally in the autumn of 1938 even
those professional men who served the
Jewish community were expelled from the
ranks of their professions. Such doctors
and lawyers might no longer call themselves
" doctors " and " lawyers " ; their degrees
were cancelled, and therewith also their
pensions, insurance and other privileges of
their profession, and their numbers were
drastically limited.

The process took five years because it was
not possible to enforce these laws completely
at the very beginning without completely
disorganizing the normal life of the country ;
but on the other hand it was sometimes found
that the exceptions permitted did not secure
the freedom from " Jewish influence " which
was desired. Thus about half the lawyers
of Berlin were Jews in 1933 (their percentage
in the country as a whole was 16 per cent.,
the highest Jewish percentage in any profession), but two-thirds of this half were

entitled to continue their practice under the exceptions for pre-war or war service. The Party was, therefore, allowed to declare this situation intolerable and simply effect a clearance of the law-courts, whatever the " legal " position of the Jewish lawyers present.

The same tactics were applied to Jewish students. Their presence at the universities was made difficult and sometimes impossible by the violence of National-Socialist student groups, whatever their legal rights to terminate their studies.

The Jews thus expelled from the professional and cultural life of the nation had little chance of turning to business or even to manual labour as an alternative, for, although the attack on the Jewish business and commercial world was organized more slowly, restrictions were introduced sufficiently early to make it impossible for many new-comers to find a livelihood in these fields. Already in May 1933 the dissolution of the Trade Unions was effected, and a National-Socialist Organization of Labour substituted, and into this organization Jews were not permitted to enter. To find an outlet in agriculture was even less possible in a state which associated so closely " blood and soil," and peasant proprietorship was restricted to those who could prove a pure "Aryan" descent back to the year 1800.

As time went on and as the attack on Jewish commercial interests was developed, the possibility of alternative employment in Germany grew more and more remote. From the very beginning spasmodic attacks on Jewish businesses had been permitted with almost complete impunity ; and it was not long before particularly prominent Jewish firms were "Aryanized." But it was not possible to make any general onslaught until German industry had been sufficiently brought under the control of the government for it to prevent the destruction of Jewish commerce from affecting the life of the country, and, on the other hand, it was not always easy to discover the location and extent of Jewish interests.

Gradually, however, the control of industrial and commercial life gave the government both the information which it required, and the means to carry out its programme. Jewish firms were gradually excluded from tendering for government contracts ; when no goods could be obtained from abroad without a government certificate, it was easy to refuse this to a Jewish business ; when the distribution of home products also was strictly rationed, supplies to Jews could easily be curtailed or simply refused ; where businesses needed licences, it was easy to cancel the licence. In all these ways, and by the punishment of Germans who dealt in Jewish shops, Jewish economic life was first diminished and then ruined. In 1938 the Government proceeded to more direct action, and simply decreed the complete exclusion of Jews from this or that occupation, the clothing trade, dealing in real estate, dealing in live-stock and so on ; and in the same year, completed its hold on the whole of Jewish economic life by the " Göring decrees " which compel every Jew to register his entire property if it is over £400, so that the government may ensure that it is " used for the greatest national advantage." As the system by which the return has to be made creates entirely mythical figures of Jewish riches, it is able both to claim to the public that the Jews still possess an enormous share of the national wealth, and to secure figures which would enable complete confiscation of the actual possessions of a Jew to appear merely as a moderate capital levy on his property—a policy already partially adopted in November 1938 to collect the fine of

£80,000,000 levied for the shooting of Vom Rath.

Since this process has been going on steadily for six years, it has naturally resulted in a continuous effort of the Jews to dispose of their rapidly dwindling businesses, but even here every kind of chicanery is practised. A Jew is fortunate if he secures for his business the wholesale price of the actual stock which he has in hand. Nothing is given for " goodwill," or the cost of his premises and fittings. In any case the ultimate price is not his to decide ; it is decided by a state commissioner who fixes it entirely in the interest of the " Aryan " who purchases it.

What has been true of business has been equally true of banking, and here the Government has complete control through the complicated system of regulations by which both currency and industrial capital are managed.

Jews who have contributed all their working life to insurances find that they are suddenly deprived of all benefits, but the money which they have paid in is not necessarily returned. Pensions are cancelled on the slightest pretext or on none. Courts have ruled again and again that contracts entered into with Jews are not binding, so that " Aryans " are given legal protection in evading their responsibilities. If the decline of his business leads to a Jew dismissing an " Aryan," the Jew can be obliged to pay him heavy compensation ; if a Jew is dismissed he has no redress at all. Sometimes a particularly humane judge will award damages to a Jew, but the Party can prevent their payment, if necessary, by the simple process of putting the Jew under arrest, " to protect him from the natural indignation which his impudent action has caused to the populace." Jews are not even left unharassed in their homes. They may not live in homes occupied by Aryans. They may not live in certain quarters of the towns, and in this way a ghetto is being recreated—but without the old ghetto's security of homogeneity.

Already by 1938 one-third of this once prosperous community was living on charity, and the proportion grows daily. It is a matter of a few years at latest to the time when the remnants of German Jewry will be totally dependent on foreign charity.

This time is brought still nearer by the removal of Jewish charities from the immunity from taxation which all registered charities enjoy. They must now pay taxes, as though they were profit-making business concerns. Jews are excluded from the

Winter Help; and the Government no longer collects for the Jewish communities the religious tax which was the method by which all religious bodies in pre-Nazi Germany were supported.

Nor has the Jewish religion been spared. In actual fact, although it is claimed that the definition of " Aryan " is purely racial, it is itself a religious definition, since all that the authorities have been able to explain about this elusive " race " is that it consists of persons none of whose grandparents professed the Jewish religion—except for " Aryan " peasants, as has been explained above. In various cities, especially Munich and Nuremberg, synagogues have been confiscated at a couple of days' notice on the flimsiest pretext, and the most exiguous compensation paid. In the pogroms of November 1938, some 500 synagogues were destroyed, including the famous synagogue in Worms, dating from the eleventh century. Fire-brigades stood by while the buildings burned—to see that neighbouring houses of " Aryans " were not involved. In many cases communities were compelled to pay for the demolition of the ruins, although they were not allowed even to receive the insurance on the destroyed buildings and their contents.

Where they still stand, synagogues and schools are taxed, although all other such religious buildings are free from taxation ; agents of the secret police attend synagogue services, and the use of Hebrew in sermons is restricted because they cannot understand it and so control what is being said ; the ritual slaughter of animals is forbidden, and the importation of meat to take its place is so restricted as to make regular supplies impossible ; in German concentration camps, and in Vienna after the Anschluss, Jewish religious observances have been made the subject of obscene " punishments." In one case the Jewish prisoners on a special day of festival were made to stand in the pit of the latrines for their service ; in Vienna, during the first weeks, it was common to make the Jews clean out the pans of barrack latrines with their praying shawls—equivalent to compelling a priest to do such work with altar and communion linen.

One result of the combined effect of all the measures described above has been the constant flight of Jews from small towns to big cities, where they hope more easily to remain hidden. Community after community has been closed down, the synagogue sold or " presented " to the authorities, the sacred scrolls removed, only the cemeteries left to recall the past ; and the towns have been able to put up the proud inscription " *JUDEN-REIN* "—free from Jews.

Parks and public gardens ; theatres, cinemas, concert halls and libraries ; health resorts and sanatoria ; sport clubs and learned societies ; one by one all these accompaniments to civilized life are closed to Jews. In return they are forced to patronize their own cultural organization—under police supervision. No play, no piece of music, no lecture can be given without it ; everything must first be submitted to the police for their approval, and if they decide arbitrarily to forbid the production there is no appeal.

In many statements of policy about the Jews, and particularly in statements made to foreign journalists, the National-Socialist Party has insisted that their entire aim is limited to the exclusion of Jews from influence in German life, since such influence is contrary to their whole racial policy. The Jews were " different," there was no question raised as to inferiority or superiority. In the same way the Government constantly asserted that everything was done " legally," and that " not a hair of the head of a Jew was injured." So far as the last statement was concerned, while it might be literally true, since hair is difficult to injure even when the head beneath is beaten bloody, there has been continuous violence against the persons of Jews all through the period. Sometimes there is a lull, sometimes an outburst, but in the quiet corners where foreigners are not likely to penetrate, in concentration camps and prisons, murders, beatings and the physical ill-treatment of individuals are continually going on.

Even worse than physical ill-treatment is the absolutely continuous stream of abuse which proceeds from government orators, especially Hitler, Goebbels and Streicher, from the radio, the newspapers and the press. This abuse is a necessary part of the campaign ; for the Germans individually are a kindly folk, and it would not have been possible to carry out the anti-Jewish policy of the Government without continually impressing on the public the bestial and diabolic nature of the whole Jewish people and their eternal hatred of the " Aryan." The fact that Jewish neighbours were usually ordinary kindly folk like themselves had to be forced out of their heads by a deafening clamour of abuse. To this end it is constantly asserted that every opposition abroad to German actions is the result of the " Jewish controlled " world press, that every nation with which she is in disagreement is dominated by Jews, that every statesman who denounces National-Socialist policy is a Jew or in Jewish pay ; and the ordinary German, who has no means of controlling the accuracy of these statements, is led ultimately to believe them, especially as he is also told that every misfortune from which he himself suffered during or after the war was directly produced by the deliberate act of his innocent-seeming Jewish neighbours.

The dignity with which the leaders of the Jewish community in Germany have met this appalling situation has been beyond all praise. Working under the constant eye of a hostile police, their every action controlled, petty difficulties set in their way at the whim of any Nazi official, they have continued at their posts, bearing a burden almost more than human being could bear. They have seen communities brought to ruin, synagogues and charitable foundations stolen from them, their funds destroyed, their archives taken away to be misused for the purpose of further campaigns against them, and all the time they have to deal with a never ending stream of individual sufferers who have been reduced, often from affluence or comfort, to absolute beggary and starvation.

The community itself has, with exceptions such as must be expected among half a million individuals, met its fate with equal dignity, and, in spite of all that is said to the contrary, it is rare to hear a refugee from Germany indulging in abuse of his late homeland. Even before the total exclusion of Jewish children from the public educational system in November 1938 money was raised for special Jewish schools where children should not be exposed to the humiliations inflicted on them by both teachers and pupils in ordinary schools (there were many exceptions to this horrible conduct, but, alas, there were still more examples of conformity to the wishes of the authorities) ; more was raised for the retraining of youth to prepare them for emigration, and still more to meet the ever-increasing number of Jews who have been made penniless. For though in many ways they have to contribute to " winter-help " and such things, they draw no benefits therefrom.

To shoulder the whole of these burdens soon became impossible, and help has had to be given by Jewish organizations outside to balance the mounting budgets of the communities. But the bulk of outside help has to be given to the refugees who succeed in escaping from the country.

At first many of them were able to bring sufficient abroad to maintain themselves, or, if the younger members left the country, their parents could send them enough to maintain them. As the years went on this became less and less possible. Not only were the Jews themselves poorer, but it became more and more difficult even for those who had money to get it or send it out of the country. To-day, apart from the special regulations governing emigration to Palestine, a Jew who sells his all at the reduced price which he is able to obtain is fortunate if, after paying all the taxes imposed on him, and surrendering all jewellery, gold and silver, he is able to take 3 per cent. of his remaining wealth abroad, and all that may be sent abroad from his own property remaining in Germany is sixteen shillings a month.

In spite of the difficulties set in the way of leaving their country, in spite of the fact that those who do so must face life in a new country almost or completely destitute, in spite of the difficulties of obtaining visas and permits to enter any other country, the flight of Jews from Germany has been continuous. In 1933 60,000 left the country, including men of world-wide reputation in science and art, literature and medicine, business and finance. By the middle of 1938 the refugees numbered well over 150,000 and some responsible students of the situation estimate the flight at over a quarter of a million.

Permanent settlement has been a matter of extraordinary difficulty. The years since 1933 have been years of widespread unemployment, and even countries which have maintained an open door for those fleeing for their lives have been unable to grant permits to work. To-day, country after country, especially the near neighbour of Germany, is compelled to refuse refugees the permission even to cross the frontier. One of the most tragic situations which has arisen since the Anschluss has been the action of the police in taking parties of refugees to the frontier and simply compelling them to cross it. No country can be expected to tolerate such abuse of international custom, and countries have felt obliged, on principle, to force the unhappy refugees to return. One group of over fifty, including old men and women and tiny children, wandered for five months up and down the Danube on a tug, being refused permission to land at any spot. Thousands lived all through the winter of 1938 in a similar plight on the German-Polish frontier. To-day the seizure of Czechoslovakia adds many thousands more to the unhappy stream of refugees, for there were many refugees already in the country, apart from the 350,000 Czechoslovak Jews.

In spite of the heroic work of Jewish organizations scarcely half of those who have left Germany can be considered to be settled in permanent quarters. Of these some 45,000 are in Palestine, 11,000 in France, 6,000 in Great Britain, and the bulk of the rest in north and south America. The United States have accepted some thousands annually, and are now opening their doors as wide as their immigration regulations permit. In addition to these there are some thousands in Great Britain and the countries of Western Europe who have been admitted on the understanding that they are seeking permanent settlement overseas.

Almost all the work of settlement has been done by Jewish organizations; the finance required has come from Jewish voluntary contributions—already more than five million pounds has been spent for the purpose. Apart from Christian subscribers to the

" Baldwin Fund " only three non-Jewish groups can claim to have made any real attempt to assist in a problem which is not only one of intense human suffering but in which more than Jewish victims are involved. For of the refugees about 15 per cent. are members of Christian denominations, and a number of these have no Jewish blood in them at all. Left-wing groups have assisted in some measure left-wing political refugees ; the academic world has given generously for the assistance of students and professors ; and the Society of Friends has been found, as always, giving unstintingly wherever there is human suffering. These three groups have given help, as have the Jewish organizations, indifferent as to whether the sufferer is Jew or Christian by religion ; of the Christian refugees it must be said that they have often found both more sympathy and more practical help in the offices of the Jewish organizations than among their own " brethren."

Once or twice in the preceding pages mention has been made of the special situation in Austria and Czechoslovakia. Tragic as has been the lot of the Jews of the old Reich, the catastrophe in these new provinces has been even greater. The former

have had five years to accustom themselves
to their altered circumstances ; the latter
were plunged suddenly into a situation which
it had taken the National-Socialists five years
to elaborate. In addition, during the first
months at any rate, every licence was given
to independent action of Party members and
subordinate leaders. In Austria especially
case after case has been proved—even in
National-Socialist courts—of bare-faced
robbery, and " confiscations " for which even
German law gave no authority. Men and
women were seized in the streets and taken
to prison without any charge being preferred,
and without any communication being
allowed with their families. Hundreds were
taken to the dreaded concentration camps in
the same way, and many are still in custody
in them. It is not surprising that with the
appearance of Hitler the figure for suicides
rises by leaps and bounds ; hundreds in
Austria were reported weekly during the
first months, and the figure is still abnormally
high.

Emigration from Austria and Czechoslovakia is even more difficult than from
Germany, since the refugee must leave the
country completely penniless, and it is not
surprising that the consulates of Vienna and

Prague have already filed applications on which it will take them many years to decide. In spite of this unhappy position individuals are seized and imprisoned and only released on giving undertakings to surrender all their property and to leave the country within impossibly short periods, when the authorities know that there is no country to which they can go. But their inability to leave the country only gives the Government an excuse to re-arrest them, and to punish them for breaking their promise. It is not surprising that almost daily the newspapers speak of shiploads of refugees being moved on from port to port in their effort to seek admission to some country or that tens of thousands are being dumped in Shanghai, not because there is any future for them there, but because it is the only place in the world where they can land without a passport.

Even if they succeed in escaping from the country, they are still not safe from Nazi activities. The Party makes no secret of its immense espionage organization overseas, or of the fact that one duty of German citizens abroad is to watch over the refugees and to report to Germany any hostile action which they may take, action for which their relations left in the country may be made to pay.

Even murders have been committed on foreign soil, and refugees living near the German frontier have been forcibly kidnapped and taken back to Germany, or else trapped into approaching the frontier where they are immediately arrested.

It is not only in this direct way that the refugees are made still to live under the shadow of the Nazi conception of Jewry. For there is also no secret as to the immense propaganda machine which is maintained throughout the world for the dissemination of Nazi race theories and the spread of antisemitism. Every year at the Party Rally at Nuremberg, representatives of antisemitic parties abroad are invited and treated as honoured guests. In 1938 a large Arab deputation were actually the guests of the German Government at Nuremberg and were given every encouragement in their struggle against the Jews—and incidentally the British Government—in Palestine.

A special office exists at Erfurt for the purpose of supplying anti-Jewish information to the foreign press, often providing it with proved forgeries such as the Protocols of the Elders of Zion, and similar " evidence." Anti-Jewish publications are distributed free in every language ; large sums of money are spent on subsidizing organizations which support the Nazi point of view, and German citizens abroad are compelled to act as agents and accept the orders of the Nazi Foreign organization. There never has been a Jewish world plot. To-day it is true to say that there is an anti-Jewish world plot, whose centre is the German Government assisted by the different organs of the National-Socialist Party.

# CHAPTER IX

OF the political conflict in Palestine, of the rival claims of Jew and Arab, and of the difficulties of the British Government as Mandatory an enormous amount is continually before the public. Of what the Jews have actually achieved in the country much less is known ; but it is only on the basis of an understanding of the place of Palestine in Jewish life in modern times that it is possible to form a judgment as to the political issues involved.

Although Palestine ceased to be the home of the bulk of the Jewish people nearly two thousand years ago, it has never lost its appeal to their emotions, and the land itself has never lacked some Jewish population. They have lived as a persecuted and despised minority under Roman, Byzantine, Crusading Christian, Saracen, and Turk. Since the rise of Islam the population, especially the rural population, has mainly consisted of Moslem Arabs, some of whom have dwelt in or roamed over the country since time immemorial.

The rise of Zionism has already been described. It resulted in the appearance in Palestine of a few colonies of Jews from Eastern Europe, whose idea was to cultivate the soil rather than be buried in it—for the older Jewish population had come to the country largely to prepare for death, and lived on the alms of the faithful collected in all parts of the Jewish world. As a matter of fact the colonies also needed considerable assistance before they really became stable, and this was given them almost entirely by Baron Edmond de Rothschild.

The first of these colonies was Rishon-le-Zion, founded in 1882; and in 1919 the total Jewish population of Palestine—including both types of Jew—amounted to about 65,000. While the final terms of the Mandate were not fixed until three years later, a movement of immigration began as soon as the frontiers were opened. From 1922 to 1924 the annual increase averaged more than 6,000; then in 1925 the flow grew suddenly to 31,000, but for the next seven years it only averaged 3,000; in 1933 the rise of National-Socialism changed it into a flood, and the annual figures were

30,000 for 1933, 42,000 for 1934, 62,000 for 1935, and 30,000 for 1936; in 1937 the beginning of serious trouble caused a slowing down of the flood, and only 10,000 were admitted.

This immigration, together with the natural increase of the population has brought the Jewish population up to about 400,000; during the same period the economic prosperity of the country has led to a considerable increase of the Arab population, which has risen in sixteen years from 650,000 to 950,000. These figures also have been swollen by immigration, some of it illegal, for the higher wages paid in Palestine have drawn to it Arabs from other countries of the Near East. As a consequence of the conditions of the Mandate it may therefore be said that a country which in 1922 supported a population of only 750,000 is now capable of supporting 1,350,000.

The control of Jewish immigration lies entirely in the hands of the Mandatory Government. Each year it fixes the total number of certificates which may be issued, and the different categories of immigrants to be admitted. While it is natural that there has been illegal immigration, especially since 1933, it would be untrue to say that this seriously modified the picture, as the authorities recognize its existence in fixing the number of certificates to issue. The basic fact is that the figure of the present Jewish population is the result of a British, not a Jewish, estimate of the number which the country can absorb. Jews have no power to enter the country except as tourists on their own decision; settlement is impossible without a certificate.

While the numbers which enter the country are controlled by external authority, the development of settlement lies entirely in Jewish hands; the full credit for the agricultural, industrial, medical, cultural and educational developments of the Palestinian Jews lies with them. They have had to purchase every inch of land which they occupy in the area within which they may settle, for, unlike biblical Palestine, the area of the Jewish Home is confined to the country west of the Jordan valley. Their colonies lie west of Jerusalem, down to the coast, up the coastal plain to Haifa, and thence through the " Valley of Jezreel," known as the " Emek," to the Sea of Galilee. It is estimated that in all the Jews own less than one-fifth of the cultivated land, although most of what they now possess was uncultivable when they purchased it ; and in purely economic terms their coming has meant the dispossession of considerably less than a thousand Arab families. This figure is British, not Jewish, for when the government was prepared to compensate such Arabs from government land some years ago, only this number could make good their claim to such a grant.

The original impetus in Palestine was naturally towards agricultural settlement ; they could not settle in the country until they purchased land, nor could they live there unless they made the land productive ; moreover, such settlement was also a symbolic reaction against the long exclusion of the Jews from the land. While Zionism is not a sentimental and romantic movement, and Jewish Palestine possesses all the aspects of a modern society, it still remains true that the agricultural colonies are one of the most remarkable achievements of the Zionist Renaissance.

There is no standard form of colony ; some are capitalist, some consist of small holdings, but the most interesting are communal settlements, worked as single units by groups which may consist of two hundred or more colonists. It is a practical not a political communism ; the workers have a common purse, common meals, common nurseries ; men and women alike work in the fields ; the children are under the care first of trained nurses and later of highly trained teachers ; they are with their parents, however, on the Sabbath, and the family life is thus preserved. The days when agricultural colonies needed the continual subsidies of " the Baron " have long since passed ; modern science and research have made every kind of rural economy possible and profitable. On what less than half a century ago were malarial swamps, sand-dunes or parched fields, there grow to-day groves of oranges and grape-fruit, fields of wheat and vegetables, and tens of thousands of young trees. Poultry and cattle are produced with yields of eggs and milk unknown before in the East. What is of particular interest is that in the neighbourhood of the Jewish settlements Arab agriculture is also slowly beginning to improve, while rich Arab landlords have almost as many acres of fruit trees as have the Jewish colonies.

The life is harder than in the cities—as it is everywhere in the world—but there are still many young Zionists whose ambitions, in their thoughts of Palestine, turn to the cultivation of its soil. The opening up of new colonies is, however, an expensive work, and agricultural colonization has not been able to keep pace with the other developments consequent on the vastly increased immigration of recent years. The Zionist ideal is : one-third of the people on the land ; one-third in industry ; one-third in the professions, public services and similar occupations. To-day little more than a third of the desired proportion on the land is achieved.

The building up of modern industry was handicapped in the early years by the lack of power. Palestine has no coal, and water power was to be found only in the Jordan Valley, where Jewish settlement did not exist. But in 1932 Pinhas Rutenberg, one of the most remarkable of Zionist pioneers, opened the great electrical works at the confluence of the Yarmuk and the Jordan, and is now able to supply all Palestine with power and light. Even the remotest colonies, while the colonists are still living in tents waiting to build their houses, are able to enjoy electric light.

The two main centres of Jewish industry are the cities of Tel Aviv and Haifa. Tel Aviv itself is one of the most extraordinary creations of Zionism, the only entirely Jewish city in the world. It arose out of a suburban settlement of Jews moving out from the Arab town and port of Jaffa ; in 1907 its site was merely sand-dunes ; to-day it has a population of over 135,000. Haifa is an older town, and not entirely Jewish, although to-day the Jews form the bulk of the population. Magnificently situated on the bay of Acre and the slopes of Mount Carmel, it possesses a number of factories, a thriving port—it is a terminus of the pipe-line from Mosul, seven hundred miles away—and a rapidly expanding commerce.

One of the most interesting of Jewish activities is the Labour Organization in which altogether some 110,000 workers are combined, making over 90 per cent. of all the workers of Palestine both intellectual and manual. This organization, called the Histadruth, performs many of the functions which in England would be the work of government departments. It secures its basic hold on the workers by the fact that it runs the labour exchange, and is able also to determine to a considerable extent the rate of wages. When almost all of the workers are its members it is almost impossible for employers to refuse its terms. In addition to these activities it runs excellent sickness insurance schemes, and, largely through the supply of first-class German refugee doctors available, is able to provide Jewish workers with the most up-to-date treatment for a modest insurance premium. In addition the Histadruth has encouraged co-operatives in the country, and controls many of them itself. Most of the 'bus services are run by it, and it has taken a considerable part in the immense activities of the building industry, competing for important government contracts, as well as for private enterprises.

The Zionist Organization has not only done wonders in the development of agricultural and industrial life in Palestine, but it has manifested anew the reality of the Jewish claim to value cultural and intellectual pursuits. Annual Jewish expenditure on education amounts to a quarter of a million a year, of which only £28,000 is provided by the Mandatory Government. Almost all the government money is spent on Arab schools, but their whole appropriation for education is less than that of the Jews. There are excellent schools in the colonies, as well as extensive libraries for the use of adults. At the crown of the whole educational system stands the University of Jerusalem, with a budget in 1936 of £90,000. Though less than twenty years old it is already an institution of first-class importance. Its research work, especially in subjects, cultural and scientific, affecting the Near East, is of as high a standard as that of any university of the world. It contains the largest library in the Near East, and among its thirty professors, as well as among its assistants and lecturers, are men who have a world-wide reputation in their own field.

The organization of this complicated venture is naturally complex. Jewish settlement in Palestine is the concern not only of the Mandatory Government and of those Jews who live in the country, but also of the Jewries of the whole world. From the standpoint of the government the official Jewish body is the Jewish Agency, a council created directly under the Mandate, and representing not merely the Zionist Organization, but also those sections of Jewry which are interested in Palestinian settlement, but do not share the political interests of the different Zionist groups. It is to the Agency that the Mandatory power hands over the certificates which it has decided to issue for immigration, and it is from the Agency that it receives complaints, requests and suggestions affecting the position of the Jews.

The Jews actually living in Palestine are

represented in an elected assembly, which, with its executive the Va'ad Leumi, performs many of the functions of an English County Council. The Va'ad Leumi is a legal body which can hold land, and levy rates on its members for educational and philanthropic purposes ; connected with it is the rabbinical court which has authority in all matters affecting religion and religious custom. It is less comprehensive in its activities than would be a County Council, for the evident reason that much of the work of upbuilding is the direct interest and the financial responsibility of Zionist Organizations outside the country. Thus, for example, two-thirds of the education work is controlled by the Zionist Educational Committee ; the best hospitals in the country, a large chain of clinics, infant welfare centres, playgrounds and similar activities which serve Jew and Arab alike are the creation of the different Women's Zionist Organizations. Money for the purchase of land is also obtained mainly outside the country, and a quarter of the land owned by the Jewish community is the permanent possession of the Jewish National Fund, which leases it to the actual settlers.

As is to be expected, the interaction of so

many different organizations in the building up of the country does not take place without friction. There are among the Jews, as among every other people, many political parties, and these parties have members both inside and outside Palestine. The Zionist Organization itself is constantly averting or failing to avert schisms within its ranks ; and party feeling runs high, both in Palestine and outside it, between the different groups. Heads are broken and windows are smashed in Warsaw as well as in Tel Aviv during Jewish party conflicts. While the strongest element in the field is the Labour Party, the " Revisionists," an almost Fascist group which demands the radical revision of the Mandate and the creation of a " state " not a " home," are sufficiently strong to be continually in evidence.

Of even greater importance than the actual achievement of Jews in building up a home in Palestine is the psychological effect of the work done on the Jewish people as a whole. It would be a complete misunderstanding of the significance of Zionism to believe that failure or success in Palestine only affected about 3 per cent. of the Jewish people because only 3 per cent. lived in Palestine. To depressed Jews all over the world there is a thrill in the fact that *Jews* have shown themselves capable of draining malarial swamps and turning them into fertile fields and olive groves ; that *Jews* have built up new and interesting forms of agricultural village life ; that they have made their own trade unions and labour councils, some of whose activities are a model to those of other countries ; that there are *Jewish* sailors manning ships owned by *Jewish* companies ; that there is one town in the world where all, from the mayor to the street scavengers, are *Jews* ; and that Hebrew is again the language of a people spoken in its streets, employed in its books and newspapers.

There is no reason why Jews should regard these facts with anything but pride, for the upbuilding of Palestine in twenty years is a unique achievement. Of course there is evidence of haste, there are rough edges ; not all the faults of life elsewhere are lost in a moment ; there is financial speculation and exploitation in Palestine as elsewhere ; there are failures as well as successes ; criminals as well as heroes and ordinary men and women ; there is a hectic quality in the life of the country ; there is a brusqueness, even an arrogance in those who have created what no one, even themselves perhaps,

believed could have been created in so short
a time. They have faced the task of
pioneers, they, the people who were said to
be unable to live except on the pioneering
of others, and have been brilliantly successful; they have built up a rich and varied
community reflecting every aspect of modern
life and reflecting it worthily; they have
dramatically and finally proved their point
that it is history and no inborn characteristic
which has made them the despised outcasts
or financial speculators of other national
communities. Even physically they have
shown an astonishing power of regeneration,
and the Palestinian born sons of the ghettoes
of Eastern Europe are sturdy peasants and
strong and skilful manual workers.

Nothing showed more completely the
solidity and the elasticity of the structure
which they had created in less than a generation than the Palestinian response to the
flight from Germany in 1933. Previously
they had had to absorb in relatively small
numbers those who came because they
longed to come, who felt themselves Palestinians long before they quitted the country
where they had been born; but in 1933 they
were asked to absorb huge groups, many of
whom still felt themselves German long after

they had actually settled in Palestine ; people who identified themselves so little with the life of the country that they wanted separate German schools for their children ; that they did not unpack all their belongings, because they would soon be returning to Germany. To absorb such successfully was a far harder task. The slow and painful realization that National Socialism was likely to last in Germany for a period of years undoubtedly assisted the process of assimilation, but the main element was the fluidity and absorptive capacity—both spiritual and economic—of the life which had already been created. So far as the Jews of Palestine themselves were concerned, they showed a capacity not merely to absorb the forty odd thousand who came, but all the Jewish population of Germany, were they allowed to do so. While other countries feared the effect on their economic life of a few hundred refugees, Palestine could absorb with profit to her economy as many thousands.

Had Palestine been an empty country, the picture could be considered complete at this point, and could end upon a note of unrelieved optimism. And even though the fact that Palestine was not empty brings a note of tragedy and failure into the colours, yet it must always be borne in mind in the subsequent pages that Zionism on its own ground has proved to the hilt the right of the Jews to independent survival and their claim to the respect of other nations.

All the problems of Zionism arise out of the fact that the Jewish National Home is not established in an independent, otherwise empty country, but is a British Mandate over a land which was already populated almost up to the limit of the capacity which the primitive and wasteful agriculture of the pre-war period allowed.

At the end of the war about eight-tenths of the population of Palestine were Moslem Arabs, one-tenth Christian Arabs and one-tenth Jews. Of the first group more than half were engaged in agriculture, working as tenants of a small semi-feudal class of landowners to whom more than three-quarters of the soil belonged. Conditions were miserable, the peasants were heavily in debt to Arab moneylenders, and when they had paid their " rent," often amounting to between one-third and one-half of their gross harvest, they had little enough to keep body and soul together. The Arab landowners did little to improve conditions, and many of them lived outside the country, collecting their rents through agents. Closely allied to the landowners was the clerical class, whose importance was much enhanced by the presence in Palestine of so many sacred Moslem sites. At the head of the Moslem population stood two clans, almost always at feud with each other, the Husseini, the family of the ex-Mufti, and the Nashashibi, that of the late Mayor of Jerusalem. The Christian Arabs were divided into the same classes, but fewer were peasants, and they constituted a higher proportion of the merchant and official classes. In positions under the Mandatory Government they actually outnumber the Moslems, although the latter are eight times as numerous in the general population.

As is to be expected in such a country corruption was the natural order of the day, and the ease with which witnesses can be obtained either by bribery or political propaganda is still a problem for the courts; the peasants also are largely illiterate and easily moved to frenzies of religious enthusiasm by skilful and unscrupulous agitation.

Finally it is worth recording that even these two " Arab " groups are by no means pure Arabs, such as are the Bedouin of the desert or the population of many of the other

Arab countries. Situated as Palestine is on a highway of the world's commerce, and of history's imperialisms, there has been a continual admixture of races in the country, and every type from negroid to "Aryan" blond can be found in the "Arab" population.

Such was the population of the country when the Balfour Declaration announced to the world the British intention to support the return of the Jews. It was made clear that the British Government did not propose in any way to prejudice the rights of the existing inhabitants; for this reason they carefully used the words "a national home *in* Palestine," and not those which the Jews would naturally have preferred, "Palestine as a national home." Their declaration was obviously based on the belief that there was room for both peoples in the country, and that the improvements introduced by the Jews would allow a much closer settlement of the land.

While, thus, in the declaration made to the Jews, the British considered that they safeguarded the rights of the Arabs, it is claimed that even this limited endorsement of Zionism ran counter to definite promises made to the Arabs during the war on various occasions and particularly in an exchange of letters between Sir Henry McMahon, High Commissioner for Egypt, and the Sherif Hussein of Mecca. In this correspondence the British Government undertook to support the Arab claims to independence from the Turks. The whole trouble comes from certain reservations in the crucial McMahon letter. In particular there were reserved from the area in which the British promised to support Arab ambitions, certain districts on the Mediterranean which were not wholly Arab, and certain districts in which the interests of France had to be considered. The phrase which the British have always claimed to include Palestine is " portions lying to the west of the districts of Damascus, Hama, etc." Geographically the claim is absurd, for even the northern frontier of Palestine lies south of Damascus, and the country as at present defined was never a single Turkish district. Politically, however, it is clear that the British *meant* the area which is now Palestine to be included, and it is also clear that Hussein and his son Feisal at the beginning were content to raise no objections. In fact in 1919 Feisal and the Zionist leader, Dr. Weizmann, signed a treaty of friendship in which Feisal conditionally approved of the

Jewish desire to return to Palestine. The condition was that the promises to the Arabs elsewhere were fulfilled.

The Jews are therefore right in saying that at the very beginning they sought Arab approval of their venture, and obtained it, for Feisal was the accepted head of the Arab delegation at Versailles. But this approval was repudiated by the Arab leaders in Palestine itself who expressed their opposition to an American Committee of Inquiry in 1919 and in an Arab delegation to London in 1921. Moreover, the conditions of the treaty were not subsequently fulfilled, in that the Arabs did not gain their independence, nor were even allowed to be united under a single " protector." France claimed Syria, and Britain Iraq and Palestine. In March 1920 Arab indignation at this betrayal of their hopes led to outbreaks in both Syria and Palestine. In the former country Feisal was proclaimed an independent king in defiance of the French and in the latter there were widespread attacks upon the Jews, who were considered to be the reason for the British refusal of Arab self-determination. A year later, in May 1921, there were still more serious riots, and this time they were due not merely to disappointed nationalism but to the fear that Jewish immigration would ruin the Arabs, and even drive them out of their country.

For eight years after 1921 an uneasy peace was maintained. The professional Arab politicians were as unreconciled as ever, but many of the Arab population came to the conclusion that compromise was possible, and that the British could be trusted to protect their interests. How brittle the peace was appeared in August 1929, when even more savage riots broke out in Jerusalem and spread throughout the country. 133 Jews were killed, and a large part of the Arab population took part in the rioting in the belief that the Jews had interfered with the most holy of Moslem Holy Places in Jerusalem. But while religious fanaticism was the ostensible cause, the riots were instigated by the same irreconcilable group of Arab politicians, and the rumours spread by them of sacrilege were the more readily believed in that opposition to Jewish immigration was growing steadily the whole time.

In 1933 a new turn was given to the conflict by disturbances which were directed not at the Jews, but at the British, and this feature has been reproduced in the disturbances which began again in 1936 and which continued, having assumed the proportions of a rebellion, until the summer of 1939.

For the first time there have been deliberate attacks on British officials, and Britain as well as, if not more than, the Jews is proclaimed to be the enemy. Many Arab moderates have been assassinated or threatened with assassination. While it is probable that outside financial assistance has had its share in rousing and arming the Arabs, while the Italians by their broadcasts from Bari, and the Germans by such expressions of sympathy as the invitation of an Arab delegation to the Party Rally at Nuremberg in 1938 have certainly exacerbated the position, yet it remains true that it is mainly the situation in the Near East itself which has caused the rebellion. In the first place the Palestinians have seen Iraq become an independent kingdom, and Syria on the threshold of the same destiny, while they are denied any form of self-government which seems to them acceptable ; in the second place they have seen Jewish immigration raise the Jewish percentage of the population from 10 to 30 ; and in the third place they have become extremely suspicious of British intentions. They have become bitter and well-informed critics of British imperialism, and at times even regard the Jews as fellow dupes with themselves.

A sinister feature of the situation is that the effects of years of propaganda are now showing themselves in that the discontent is no longer confined to a small and educated class, but is widespread throughout the whole population, especially amongst the younger generation who have never known Turkish rule. The grievances, however, although more widely felt, still remain entirely political. The Arab nationalists have never attempted to propose schemes of economic or educational betterment, and the unrest is no result of the refusal of such schemes. In actual fact the Mandatory Government has done far more for the poor Arab than have their own leaders ; the Jews also, with their free hospitals and clinics, and with their fight for better conditions for workers of all classes, could make an equally justifiable claim to have done more for the Arabs than the Grand Mufti and all the other leaders of the extremists. But Arab agitation does not rest on facts ; it rests on fears and on those imponderables which often count more than facts in the lives of nations, especially at a time of universal nationalism such as the present.

The Arab fear is the simple one that in time the Jew will dominate the country entirely, and leave him only in the position of a tolerated and outclassed alien. Although official statements have often been made, and made with perfect sincerity, by the Zionist Organization that they desire to share the country with the Arabs and "neither to dominate nor be dominated," yet the Arab fears are understandable enough. Political nationalism is inextricably bound up with cultural idealism and human sympathy in the different Jewish parties. There is the ancient statement of Dr. Weizmann, made in 1919, that he considered the Balfour Declaration to mean that Palestine would be Jewish in the sense that England was English ; there is the arrogant behaviour of individual Jewish settlers, who assume that they are the owners of the country—a small point in itself, and very natural when the settler has exchanged the misery of Poland for the free air of Palestine, but extremely irritating to others,—there is the continual demand for ever more and more immigration certificates, and the indignation at anything put in the way of the extension of the National Home ; there is the belief that the Jews of Palestine have behind them in London and elsewhere a power infinitely greater than that possessed by the Palestinian Arabs, so that attention is never given to the latter's case ; and there is the fear of a more backward civilization that it will be swallowed up in a more active and progressive one. All these fears can be resumed in the single demand for independence or at least the abandonment of the idea of the Jewish National Home. The Arabs are not interested in whether they would have better standards of living under Jewish domination ; they are not interested in Britain's imperial commitments, and her desire to control pipe-lines and air-ports. They claim that Palestine is their country, and they want to govern it themselves in their own way. This was their case in 1919, and this is their case, put much more forcibly, to-day ; for if in 1919 the Jews were only 10 per cent., already they are 30 per cent., and are demanding wider doors to immigration. To-morrow they fear that it may be their country no longer, that the Jews will be, as they so constantly claim they have a right to be, the actual majority of the population.

The historian may regard this as a classical example of the disease of nationalism ; he may be convinced that every argument of reason and of pity is on the Jewish side, but the statesman and the politician are compelled to accept the situation which they find. Even British responsibility for allowing the disease to spread cannot alter the existing situation. The disease is there, and any solution has to take it into account.

The Jews on their side are equally intransigent, and can make a better legal showing for their attitude. For if it is uncertain whether the Arabs have any justification in claiming that they were promised independence, the Jews were certainly given the Balfour Declaration, and it was doubly confirmed, first by the Allied Powers, and later by the United States and the Council of the League of Nations. But while this claim is legally unimpeachable it shows little understanding of political realities for Jews continually to reiterate that they are only demanding, and must be given, their legal rights.

From the time when the Mandate was drawn up until the British-Jewish and British-Arab Conferences in the Spring of 1939 the British Government has attempted to accept the basis of the Mandate and to reconcile it with the claims of the Arabs. One Commission has followed another, and, whether through their own fault or not, none have provided a solution. Now at last another pronouncement has been made, limiting immigration to 75,000 in five years, after which it can only be continued with Arab approval, and providing for an evolution to a possible independence in ten years.

What the future of this will be it is still impossible to say, as in August 1939 the Mandates Commission of the League of Nations refused to accept it as a legitimate interpretation of the Mandate, and though their function is officially only advisory, it is unlikely that the British will be able successfully to carry through a policy so publicly condemned by a neutral international body.

It is less surprising that the Zionists have seen in the pronouncement nothing but the betrayal of a binding legal obligation to continue indefinitely the protection and promotion by immigration of the Jewish National Home.

The whole position is extremely complicated. In the first place no political promise can be permanently binding entirely independent of altered circumstances. We are realizing to-day the folly of considering the Treaty of Versailles to be eternal, and of refusing to amend its more glaring faults in time.

There is no reason why the Balfour Declaration should be on a different footing. The British Government can legitimately argue that the circumstances have so altered that it is no longer possible to carry it out, as indeed the Royal Commission of 1937 declared in no uncertain language. Both the British and the Jews hoped that the Arabs would accept the Jewish Home ; the hope has proved fallacious, to whomsoever be ascribed the fault, and it is not unreasonable to claim that to continue to try and apply the Declaration has become immoral.

In the second place the Declaration is itself vague. At what statistical point does a National Home become a National Home, so that the promise might be considered to be redeemed ? Is the test economic or political ? The answer depends not merely on geography but on human actions and reactions. On the one hand the Jews have shown that " absorptive " capacity entirely depends on planned economy ; but on the other hand it is difficult to see what answer can be given when the Government says : " The country is as full as the present political position will stand. There must be a limit to immigration until it can be continued with the agreement of the Arabs."

It was easy to foretell what the Jewish reaction to such a pronouncement would be, and this introduces the third point. At the time when the Declaration was made, and at the time when the Mandate was drawn up, it could not have been foreseen that the life of the Jewish people elsewhere would pass from tragedy to tragedy, until Palestine appeared the only bright spot upon an otherwise black horizon. It has already been shown with what high hopes Jews entered the post-war world. The National Home had a spiritual, a cultural, significance ; it was not thought of as a refuge from persecution and starvation, a dump for the unwanted Jews of other countries. The Jews cannot be blamed for their demand that the Mandate be carried out and that the only limit set to immigration should be their capacity to absorb the immigrants, so long as there are fellow-Jews in desperate need and with nowhere else to go. The surge of pity is probably far stronger to-day than any political ambition ; and it is one of the greatest tributes to the success of Zionism that it has so successfully absorbed and welded together the unexpected elements which Jewish settlement has come to include. But it still remains true that the Balfour

Declaration was never meant to be an authority for compelling the Palestinian Government to accept in ever increasing quantities the victims of persecution elsewhere.

Had there been a slow upbuilding with ample time to conciliate the Arabs, to allow the extremists to appear for the empty and lying agitators which they so often were, it is at least possible that the situation now would be so totally different that a tragedy, such as that which has befallen the Jews of Germany, would have moved the emotions of the Arab as it has moved the emotions of the rest of the world, so that he would have been willing to receive even larger numbers of those whom he had learnt by experience to be good and useful neighbours.

Whatever its advantages, the Balfour Declaration has been a tragedy from one point of view. It has obscured from the rank and file of the Zionist Movement, if not from the leaders, the stark truth that the ultimate success of the National Home is its acceptance by the Arabs. Far too much reliance has been placed on its words, and on British bayonets and British imperial interests to enforce them. Much criticism can be levelled at the Mandatory Government, and at the Colonial Office which ultimately directs it, and the last Royal Commission was very open in such criticisms, but, whatever the faults of the British, that remains true. In its final analysis the success of the National Home must be based on harmonious Jewish-Arab relations, whatever the price at which they are achieved. And if this were once accepted as fundamental by Zionism, the White Paper of May 1939 might still prove the turning-point to a new era.

# EPILOGUE

## THE FUTURE

I have avoided the use of " I " up to this point, for, although every book is but the expression of the mind of its author, yet I have desired to give the facts of the present position of the Jews together with as much of their history as is necessary, as objectively and impersonally as possible. But when I turn to the future, I have no facts to speak for themselves, and it would be the sheerest pedantry to pretend that I give anything but a personal impression, conditioned by my own beliefs and related to my own philosophy of life.

In its heroism and its sordidness, its grandeur and its pettiness, its optimism and disillusion, its shortsightedness and its infinite patience, the drama of Jewish history is unique, not in the sense of being apart from the experience of other peoples, but as an epitome and microcosm of the whole striving of humanity. It differs in intensity, not in kind, from the stories of others. But although Jewry has known many times of distress in the four thousand years of its existence, never has a century and a half been so crowded with experience as the period which stretches from the emancipation in France in 1789 down to the present day. In that brief period have been crowded together the heady wine of citizenship, the seductive dream of complete assimilation, the shock of reborn antisemitism, the uprooting of a quarter of the whole people, the hopes for an end to persecution, and the coming of a persecution more bitter and relentless than any previously endured, the joy of return to Palestine, and the discovery of unlooked-for obstacles to the rebirth of the nation.

In previous periods when there was persecution in one centre, there was prosperity in another ; poverty was balanced by wealth, moral decay by moral regeneration. To-day it seems that everywhere the same phenomena are being repeated. Nowhere is antisemitism on the decline, nowhere is Jewish life becoming easier and more prosperous. In the Middle Ages the ghetto gates shut out the enemy as effectively as they shut in the Jew. To-day, for worse as well as for better, the ghetto gates are down.

Germany, which has set him in a ghetto of her own inventing, has denied him that one humane alleviation which the Middle Ages granted. Even in the Synagogue the agent of the secret police has the right to be present.

Wherever I turn in surveying the contemporary Jewish scene, the colours are sombre, the horizons dark, but I fear that there is still worse to come ; the last act of the tragedy is not yet upon the stage.

In estimating the chance of survival one point needs to be taken into account. The Jewish people has, as I have shown, been deformed by the history through which they have passed. They are to-day an abnormal people, and there are real problems involved in their adjustment to the community. But while they are being so violently attacked, while such exaggerated nonsense is talked about them, they cannot but spend most of their energies in defence and have little time for readjustment. It is difficult even to expect them to admit their faults when the slightest admission is immediately seized on as a justification for their complete segregation or extermination.

Must the last act, then, be the destruction of the Jewish people ? That they have survived so long is not necessarily proof that they will always survive. On the other hand survival will depend on themselves, not on their enemies. Tradition will carry them a long way, but survival must mean that there are continually recreative forces in contemporary Jewish life. Do these exist?

I believe that the strongest such force is Zionism. Inevitably in an age of chauvinistic nationalism, Zionism has a chauvinistic side. Revisionism will flourish as long as the atmosphere is full of nationalism of its type; then it will wilt and die as all such movements in Jewish history have died, from the time when Solomon and Jeroboam caught the fever of imperialism from their neighbours onwards. But chauvinistic nationalism is not the heart of Zionism. It is important for the Gentile to realize that Zionism is essentially a movement of spiritual and cultural renaissance, even though religious Judaism is little in evidence in the Zionist settlement in Palestine.

At the present moment Zionism is tragically distracted from its main task by the appalling need for finding a home for tens of thousands of unhappy exiles. So long as the rest of the world closes its doors, so long will, and must, Jews devote their main strength to demanding the maximum possibilities for emigration to Palestine—whatever the Arab opposition. But the main task of Zionism is not even in Palestine ; it is wherever Jews are living. Palestine is the centre, and as such it is of vital importance. But a centre is nothing without a circumference. Even if Palestine collapsed, through Arab opposition and British inability to hold the position, the task of Zionism would not be finished. There is an interesting parallel in Jewish history itself. Pharisaism arose largely as a movement for the correct performance of the Temple ritual. It builded so well that, when the Temple fell, Pharisaism hardly felt a ripple on its surface. I trust that Zionism will not be put to so terrible a test, but if it were, I believe that, after a brief period of utter despair, it would rise to its task.

Most of my Jewish friends regard Zionism and Assimilationism as irreconcilable opposites. I think they are wrong. Zionist and Assimilationist in the curious life of the Jewish people are as necessary to each other as Conservative and Labour in English political life. They represent the two components, both of which are necessary, but which we cannot yet fuse together. The Assimilationist is the necessary interpreter of

Jewish experience to the Gentile world, speaking from within the group of which he is a Jewish member ; and he is also the necessary carrier to the Jewish nationalist of the cultural environment in which he lives. Zionist enthusiasm was born in the narrow confines of a ghetto life ; its realization in Palestine was only possible because of all that Jewry had assimilated in the nineteenth-century world. It is a great mistake to think that Jewish history has thrived on separation. Abraham grew out of the assimilation of the wisdom of Ur, and Moses out of assimilating the wisdom of Egypt. But they were a notable pair of " Zionists " ! It is equally true to put it the other way round. Abraham led his tribe to Palestine from the east, Moses from the south, but they were a notable pair of Assimilationists !

I believe that the Jews will survive, because these two elements are healthy—especially when they get angry with each other !

But the survival is going to be at a cost. There is stark tragedy facing the Jews of Germany, Poland, and to a lesser extent of other countries of Eastern Europe. And I do not believe that many Jews will survive in Russia, except as accidental descendants of a particular extinct group. In all these cases some unexpected event may alter the picture, but there is no sign to-day of where or how such an alteration might come.

The Jews will survive, but for a period antisemitism will make their lives still more difficult than they are now. There are no signs of a decrease of that disease, and as long as it remains an essential element in the policies of a rich and powerful nation, so long will antisemitic agitators lack neither funds nor material. On the other hand, the very excesses and the scientific absurdities of modern racial antisemitism justify the belief that there will be an equally strong reaction when the motive force has passed. And I have always felt that the prophets of National-Socialism are unduly optimistic when they proclaim that their regime will last ten thousand years. I do not think the Jews will have to wait as long as that.

While German support and not yet out-grown Jewish deformities will keep anti-semitic agitation flourishing for some while yet, there are signs that the forces making for understanding, though at present under an eclipse, are growing.

In the first place time is on the side of the Jews. The immigrants from Germany may, as has been said, all carry seeds of antisemitism in their baggage, however slender it may be, but the general slowing down of migration is allowing the Jewish populations of western countries to adjust themselves better to their environment than did either the assimilationists of the first period of emancipation or the immense groups of fugitives from Russia before the war.

In the second place those who believe in democracy are beginning to realize that anti-semitism is an expensive luxury which they cannot afford. Of course democrats may go on disliking Jews individually, but they are beginning to see that there are things which they dislike much more. And when the Jewish question is reduced to dislike of those Jews who have done something to deserve it, its sting is drawn.

In the third place there are the faint beginnings of a new attitude of Christians to Jews, especially in Britain and America. There is the beginning of a realization that Judaism and Christianity stand or fall together as beliefs in a world of ultimate values where might is not always right; there is the beginning of a realization that their ethics are the same ethics—and that their God is the same God.

These last two reasons are of particular

importance. The Jew will survive by his own inner force ; but he cannot cease to provide a " problem " without non-Jewish co-operation. Nowhere is the Jew master of his own fortune. Neither in Russia nor in Poland, in Germany nor in Palestine can he make his own decisions and determine his own destiny upon them. And in the democratic countries he can only exercise the virtue of hospitality to the homeless in so far as rigid immigration laws permit.

There is no prosperity for the Jew until the virtue of toleration recovers its honour among men. Totalitarianism and nationalism cannot be tolerant of differences, but it is a disease to see in difference a danger instead of a potential enrichment. The recent adherence of Italy to the philosophic theories of Germany, theories which she ridiculed only a few years ago, shows how inevitably totalitarianism comes to resent the presence of the Jew, however closely he may be identified in loyalty and interest with the majority. There is the quite different totalitarianism of Russia, who proclaims that she has abolished antisemitism, and that the Jews enjoy complete freedom. They do indeed enjoy freedom—to speak Yiddish and not to be massacred ; but it seems to me that what is prohibited of the Jewish inheritance is far more than what is allowed. I believe that the result in Russia can only be that " the operation was completely successful but unfortunately the patient died."

The other virtue which must return to favour before a change in Jewish fortunes can take place is generosity. There cannot be peace in Palestine until the Jews have time to think of other things than the immediate placing of as many homeless refugees as the Mandatory Power can be persuaded to admit, but how can the Jews cease to concentrate on this point until some other home is opened ? I very much doubt whether the present policy of closed doors is really economically justifiable. Historically, at any rate, countries have profited and not lost from the admission of refugees, and there are many ways in which their advent would accelerate and not retard the wheels of economic recovery.

There can be no alleviation of the tragedy in Poland until the doors of immigration are opened—both to Poles and Jews, for it must not be forgotten that tens of thousands of Poles emigrated annually before the war, and that this movement has ceased as well as the movement of Jews. It is not only unfair but foolish to imagine that the Poles can solve their problems just by compelling Jews to emigrate. If restrictions were removed they are far more likely to be removed in favour of peasants accustomed to the land, than for the purpose of swelling the numbers of the urban unemployed. But emigration cannot solve the whole problem, nor is there any justice in demanding the emigration of Jews who have lived in a country for centuries, and contributed to the growth of its economy and its traditions. The primitive selfishness of all Nationalisms, the Polish included, is extraordinarily shortsighted, but so long as it remains the policy of a government and of powerful antisemitic parties to exclude the Jews from every possible kind of honourable employment, so long will Jewish misery increase. Private charity cannot possibly cope with the steady decline to below the subsistence level of millions of people.

It is obvious that the decline in generosity is a phenomenon of a limping economic system, so that the truth is again apparent that the Jews cannot alter their own destiny. As they are dependent on the recovery of democracy, so they are dependent on the return of prosperity.

There is no more curious phenomenon in the whole subject than the fact that there are still apparently reasonable people who are convinced that the Jews secretly control the financial destinies of the world, and even sway the policies of the nations, when every fact proclaims their helplessness. If there is any truth in the belief that Jews are exceptionally intelligent, it is difficult to see how they can also have deliberately created a situation which has brought more misery on themselves than on anyone else.

There are, of course, rich Jews, and we should be grateful that it is so. For almost all that has been done to alleviate the situation has been done with Jewish money. Few people realize the extent of the burden which Jewry bears. I remember discussing the situation with an old Jewish friend, and quite casually he made the remark: "I can rarely meet my communal obligations with less than a third of my income." And he was not a rich man. The sum which the Jews of England have raised to help Jewish refugees from Germany amounts to an average of more than £4 per head of the Jewish population of this country. The average amount which Christians have raised for Christian refugees from the same country is considerably less than a penny. Generosity is certainly a virtue which we have not to teach the adherents of that religion which Christian pulpits continually proclaim to be soulless and legalistic.

All this means that the struggle against antisemitism will be a long struggle. But there is a final and rather horrible reason why I see no immediate likelihood of an alleviation of Jewish misery. The world has been so buffeted by tragedy that it has grown numb. The victims of the ruthlessness of modern Nationalism, whether in Germany or China, in Spain or in Abyssinia are so innumerable that the springs of liberality are dried up by the hopelessness of ever coping with a tithe, nay a hundredth part, of the problem. And that which would once have stirred a whole nation to indignation and to practical sympathy now passes almost unnoticed in a two-inch paragraph in the less important pages of a daily paper. There is little enough reason to hope that a world which deserted Abyssinia, China and Czechoslovakia will have its conscience finally stirred to action by refusal to desert the Jews.

Moreover the task of the non-Jews is not merely passing resolutions of sympathy and protest ; of indulging in philosemitic utterances as extravagant as those of the anti-semites. It is a question of facing facts with them, and honestly seeking together a solution. It is a question of patience and understanding and knowledge, and, where the need is, of action.

The Jew will always be in danger of finding himself the scapegoat of national and social hysteria, but sanity will yet return to the world, and moral principles are eternal ; and in any civilization which is founded on moral concepts antisemitism is a measure not of Jewish failings, but of Gentile failure.

# BIBLIOGRAPHY

*A Short History of the Jewish People, 1600 B.C.–A.D. 1935*, by Cecil Roth. Macmillan, 1936. 443 pages. 18s.

> A short bibliography on pages 427–8. The fourth part, " Twilight," provides an excellent background for students wishing to understand the background of emancipation.

*The Jewish Problem*, by Louis Golding. A Penguin Special. 1938. 213 pages. 6d.

> A history of Jewish-Gentile relationships with special stress on the post-Emancipation period.

*The Jew and His Neighbour*. A study of the causes of Anti-Semitism, by James Parkes. 2nd edition. Student Christian Movement Press, 1938. 182 pages. 3s. 6d.

> An analysis of the religious, economic and politico-racial elements in the Jewish question, and a study of their effects on Jewish life.

*Anti-Semitism Historically and Critically Examined*, by Hugo Valentin. Translated from the Swedish by A. G. Chater. V. Gollancz, 1936. 324 pages. 10s. 6d.

> Deals particularly with the accusations made against Jewry in the post-War period. With full references to sources.

*The Jews in the Modern World*, by Arthur Ruppin. 2nd edition. Macmillan, 1934. 423 pages. 15s.

> An exhaustive sociological study of the present Jewish situation, by a leading authority. With many statistics.

*Jewish Life in Modern Times*, by Israel Cohen. 2nd
edition. Methuen, 1934. 350 pages. 12s. 6d.
> The social, political, economic, intellectual, religious,
> and national aspects of present-day Jewry.

*The House that Hitler Built*, by Stephen H. Roberts.
10th edition. Methuen, 1938. 408 pages. 12s. 6d.
> An unbiased account of the new Germany by an
> Australian professor, based on first-hand experience
> gained during a prolonged stay in the country.
> Part IV, Chapter VII, deals with " The Present
> Place of the Jews."

*Six Years of Hitler* : The Jews under the Nazi regime,
by G. Warburg. Allen and Unwin, 1939. 317
pages. 7s. 6d.
> A balanced and fully documented account.

*The Refugee Problem.* Report of a survey, by Sir John
Hope Simpson. Oxford University Press, 1938.
637 pages. 25s.
> The most detailed study yet made of the refugee
> problem. The author was responsible for the
> resettlement of the Greek refugees from Asia Minor
> and other work of this kind since 1923. Well
> documented. Deals also with non-Jewish refugees.

*You and the Refugee*, by Norman Angell and Dorothy
F. Buxton. A Penguin Special. 1939. 279
pages. 6d.

> An investigation of the reasons for and against the
> admission of refugees.

*Report of the Palestine Royal Commission.* July 1937.
(Cmd. 5479.) Stationery Office, 1937. 404 pages.
6s. 6d.
> Report of the Commission sent out under the chair-
> manship of Earl Peel to Palestine to ascertain the
> causes of the disturbances since 1936 and to investi-
> gate into the state of the country generally. Most
> useful for its historical analysis of the situation.

## BIBLIOGRAPHY

*Statement of Policy on Palestine*. May 1939. (Cmd. 6019.) Stationery Office, 1939. 12 pages. 2*d*.

> The White Paper laying down the proposals of the Government.

*Palestine on the Eve*, by Ladislas Farago. Putnam, 1936. 286 pages. 10*s*. 6*d*.

> The situation at the beginning of the riots as seen by a Hungarian journalist.

*Fulfilment in the Promised Land, 1917–37*. By Norman Bentwich. Soncino Press, 1938. 246 pages. 8*s*. 6*d*.

> An appraisement of the achievements of Zionism since the Balfour Declaration, by a leading Zionist.

*No Ease in Zion*, by T. R. Feiwel. Secker and Warburg, 1938. 365 pages. 12*s*. 6*d*.

> A brilliant analysis of the growth of Zionism and of the present position, from the pen of a young Jewish Socialist.

*Common Ground*. A plea for intelligent Americanism, by Morris L. Lazaron. New York, Liveright Publishing Co., 1938. 328 pages. 10*s*. 9*d*.

> The views of an American Jew on current Jewish Problems from the non-Zionist standpoint.

# INDEX

Printed in Great Britain by Butler & Tanner Ltd., Frome and London

# THE
# HOME UNIVERSITY LIBRARY
## OF MODERN KNOWLEDGE

## Literature

## Political and Social Science

## Religion and Philosophy

# Science

*Complete List up to August 1939. New titles will be added yearly.*